Gambling

OPPOSING VIEWPOINTS®

Gambling

OPPOSING VIEWPOINTS®

Other Books of Related Interest

Gambling

OPPOSING VIEWPOINTS®

James D. Torr, *Book Editor*

Daniel Leone, *President*

Bonnie Szumski, *Publisher*

Scott Barbour, *Managing Editor*

OPPOSING
VIEWPOINTS®
SERIES

GREENHAVEN PRESS
SAN DIEGO, CALIFORNIA

GALE GROUP

THOMSON LEARNING

Detroit • New York • San Diego • San Francisco
Boston • New Haven, Conn. • Waterville, Maine
London • Munich

Cover photo: © CORBIS

Library of Congress Cataloging-in-Publication Data

Gambling : opposing viewpoints / James D. Torr, book editor.
    p. cm. — (Opposing viewpoints series)
    Includes bibliographical references and index.
    ISBN 0-7377-0906-5 (pbk. : alk. paper) —
ISBN 0-7377-0907-3 (lib. : alk. paper)
    1. Gambling. I. Torr, James D., 1974– . II. Opposing
viewpoints series (Unnumbered)

HV6710 .G3143 2002
306.4'82—dc21   2001051246

Copyright © 2002 by Greenhaven Press,
an imprint of The Gale Group
10911 Technology Place, San Diego, CA 92127

"Congress shall make no law. . . abridging the freedom of speech, or of the press."

First Amendment to the U.S. Constitution

The basic foundation of our democracy is the First Amendment guarantee of freedom of expression. The Opposing Viewpoints Series is dedicated to the concept of this basic freedom and the idea that it is more important to practice it than to enshrine it.

Contents

Why Consider Opposing Viewpoints?

"The only way in which a human being can make some approach to knowing the whole of a subject is by hearing what can be said about it by persons of every variety of opinion and studying all modes in which it can be looked at by every character of mind. No wise man ever acquired his wisdom in any mode but this."

John Stuart Mill

In our media-intensive culture it is not difficult to find differing opinions. Thousands of newspapers and magazines and dozens of radio and television talk shows resound with differing points of view. The difficulty lies in deciding which opinion to agree with and which "experts" seem the most credible. The more inundated we become with differing opinions and claims, the more essential it is to hone critical reading and thinking skills to evaluate these ideas. Opposing Viewpoints books address this problem directly by presenting stimulating debates that can be used to enhance and teach these skills. The varied opinions contained in each book examine many different aspects of a single issue. While examining these conveniently edited opposing views, readers can develop critical thinking skills such as the ability to compare and contrast authors' credibility, facts, argumentation styles, use of persuasive techniques, and other stylistic tools. In short, the Opposing Viewpoints Series is an ideal way to attain the higher-level thinking and reading skills so essential in a culture of diverse and contradictory opinions.

In addition to providing a tool for critical thinking, Opposing Viewpoints books challenge readers to question their own strongly held opinions and assumptions. Most people form their opinions on the basis of upbringing, peer pressure, and personal, cultural, or professional bias. By reading carefully balanced opposing views, readers must directly confront new ideas as well as the opinions of those with whom they disagree. This is not to simplistically argue that everyone who reads opposing views will—or should— change his or her opinion. Instead, the series enhances readers' understanding of their own views by encouraging confrontation with opposing ideas. Careful examination of others' views can lead to the readers' understanding of the logical inconsistencies in their own opinions, perspective on why they hold an opinion, and the consideration of the possibility that their opinion requires further evaluation.

Evaluating Other Opinions

To ensure that this type of examination occurs, Opposing Viewpoints books present all types of opinions. Prominent spokespeople on different sides of each issue as well as well-known professionals from many disciplines challenge the reader. An additional goal of the series is to provide a forum for other, less known, or even unpopular viewpoints. The opinion of an ordinary person who has had to make the decision to cut off life support from a terminally ill relative, for example, may be just as valuable and provide just as much insight as a medical ethicist's professional opinion. The editors have two additional purposes in including these less known views. One, the editors encourage readers to respect others' opinions—even when not enhanced by professional credibility. It is only by reading or listening to and objectively evaluating others' ideas that one can determine whether they are worthy of consideration. Two, the inclusion of such viewpoints encourages the important critical thinking skill of objectively evaluating an author's credentials and bias. This evaluation will illuminate an author's reasons for taking a particular stance on an issue and will aid in readers' evaluation of the author's ideas.

It is our hope that these books will give readers a deeper understanding of the issues debated and an appreciation of the complexity of even seemingly simple issues when good and honest people disagree. This awareness is particularly important in a democratic society such as ours in which people enter into public debate to determine the common good. Those with whom one disagrees should not be regarded as enemies but rather as people whose views deserve careful examination and may shed light on one's own.

Thomas Jefferson once said that "difference of opinion leads to inquiry, and inquiry to truth." Jefferson, a broadly educated man, argued that "if a nation expects to be ignorant and free . . . it expects what never was and never will be." As individuals and as a nation, it is imperative that we consider the opinions of others and examine them with skill and discernment. The Opposing Viewpoints Series is intended to help readers achieve this goal.

David L. Bender and Bruno Leone,
Founders

Greenhaven Press anthologies primarily consist of previously published material taken from a variety of sources, including periodicals, books, scholarly journals, newspapers, government documents, and position papers from private and public organizations. These original sources are often edited for length and to ensure their accessibility for a young adult audience. The anthology editors also change the original titles of these works in order to clearly present the main thesis of each viewpoint and to explicitly indicate the opinion presented in the viewpoint. These alterations are made in consideration of both the reading and comprehension levels of a young adult audience. Every effort is made to ensure that Greenhaven Press accurately reflects the original intent of the authors included in this anthology.

Introduction

*"Play not for gain, but sport; who plays for more than he
can lose with pleasure stakes his heart."*

—George Herbert

Americans love to gamble. More than half of all adults say
they play the lottery, and more than a quarter regularly frequent casinos, according to a 1999 National Opinion Research Center study. Each year Americans lose more than
$50 billion on legal wagering in casinos and bingo halls, on
lotteries, and at racetracks. They spend an additional un-
known amount in private settings, such as poker games, and
through illegal channels, such as bookies. "Judging by dollars spent," writes Timothy L. O'Brien in his book *Bad Bet*,
"gambling is now more popular in America than baseball,
the movies, and Disneyland—*combined*."

This enthusiasm for gambling is as old as the nation itself.
During the Revolutionary War, states sponsored lotteries to
help finance their armies. Thomas Jefferson advocated state-
sponsored gambling as a voluntary, rather than a coercive,
tax. Lotteries became popular again after the Civil War,
when southern states used them to finance Reconstruction
projects. Lotteries were sanctioned because they raised
funds for worthy causes; other forms of gambling remained
illegal and socially unacceptable until the twentieth century.

Many states started to permit betting on horse and dog
races in the 1920s, and Nevada became the first state to legalize casino-style gambling in 1931. Every state had banned
lotteries because of scandals in the 1880s involving embezzlement and fraud, but in 1964 New Hampshire, which has
no income or sales tax, revived the lottery as a means of generating revenue. It was an enormous success, with the majority of tickets purchased by out-of-state residents. "In the
next ten years," writes economics professor Richard Mc-
Gowan, "every northeastern state approved a lottery." But,
he reports, "the greatest growth of state lotteries occurred
between 1980 and 1990. Twenty-five states approved lotteries, offtrack betting, keno, and video poker machines."

However, the 1990s may be remembered as the decade in which Americans truly embraced gambling. In 1993, for the first time in U.S. history, revenues from casino gambling were greater than those from state lotteries. According to McGowan, "this marked a turning point: Casino gambling became the preferred form of gambling in the United States. It also marked the acceptance of gambling as a legal source of entertainment."

One reason for this was the enormous growth that Las Vegas experienced in the early 1990s. Tourism jumped by 24 percent in this period, and by 1996 the city's population was almost four times what it had been in 1980. This was in part because the gambling mecca had pursued a massive public relations campaign, downplaying its image as "Sin City" and instead marketing itself as a family-friendly vacation desti-nation. Casinos such as the MGM Grand, for example, built roller coasters and theme parks in addition to slot machines and craps tables, and the $900 million Mirage casino-resort created an all-ages tropical theme park in the middle of the desert. Another factor in the city's growth was the lure of slot machines, one of the most popular forms of gambling: In 1983, revenue from slot machines surpassed that of other games, such as blackjack or roulette, for the first time.

Another important development in the 1990s was the spread of Indian casinos. Many American Indian reservations are on lands that lack natural resources, and poverty and un-employment are exceptionally high among Native Americans. In the 1980s many tribes looked to casino gambling as a means of generating both jobs and tribal revenues. In 1987 the Supreme Court ruled that tribes could operate legal forms of gambling on their lands free from state regulation and taxes. In response to criticism of the large amounts of untaxed, uncontrolled income, Congress passed the Indian Gaming Regulatory Act, which returned some power to states. The re-sult has been a compromise, with tribes and state govern-ments negotiating over whether a tribe may build a casino and what types of games it may offer. Today there are more than 120 Indian casinos in 28 states. The most successful of these has been the Mashantucket Pequots' Foxwoods Resort Casino in Connecticut, which is the world's largest casino.

Several states have tried to emulate the success of Las Vegas and some Indian casinos. Iowa became the first state to legalize riverboat gambling in 1989. Over the next few years, other states along the Mississippi River also legalized riverboat gambling in order to compete for revenues, just as northeastern states had adopted lotteries in order to compete with New Hampshire. Towns as unlikely as Deadwood, South Dakota; Joliet, Illinois; and Detroit, Michigan, have all approved gambling in the hope that it will provide economic benefits. As of 2001, only Utah and Hawaii do not have some form of legalized gambling.

Not surprisingly, the spread of legalized gambling has raised a number of concerns. Many Americans remain morally opposed to gambling. The Navajo, for example, have refused to adopt Indian casinos on ethical grounds. Others warn about the growing problem of compulsive gambling, which in some cases can lead to bankruptcy, crime, and even suicide. Some critics charge that it is wrong for the government to promote gambling and unwise for states to rely on gambling for revenue. A growing antigambling movement, headed by organizations such as the National Coalition Against Legalized Gambling, maintains that the social costs of gambling far outweigh its purported economic benefits.

In 1997, President Bill Clinton appointed the National Gambling Impact Study Commission (NGISC) to address these concerns. The commission released its report in June 1999. The report is inconclusive on many important issues, stating that "the available information on economic and social impact is spotty at best and usually inadequate for an informed discussion." The commission did, however, call for a moratorium on gambling expansion. "The Commissioners believe it is time to consider a pause in the expansion of gambling," the report states. "The purpose of this recommended pause is to encourage governments to do what to date few if any have done: To survey the results of their decisions and to determine if they have chosen wisely."

As the NGISC report indicates, the debate over legalized gambling is far from over. *Gambling: Opposing Viewpoints* explores the issue in the following chapters: Is Gambling Immoral? How Serious Is the Problem of Compulsive Gambling? How Does Legalized Gambling Affect Communities? How Should the Government Regulate Gambling? Because legalized gambling has become so widespread, it is important to consider what the full social and economic impacts of gambling will be. The viewpoints in this book have been selected to introduce the reader to this ongoing debate.

CHAPTER 1

Is Gambling Immoral?

Chapter Preface

The millions of Americans who flock to Las Vegas, Atlantic City, and dozens of smaller gambling venues often say that gambling is just another form of entertainment—they view their time at a casino as no more wrong than a night at the movies or a weekend at the beach. University of Nevada English professor Felicia Campbell even argues that gambling is a spiritually uplifting experience: Gambling is "part of 'the adventurer within us,'" she writes, "yet we treat gambling as the Victorians treated sex."

Holding the opposite view are leaders such as Ralph Reed, former director of the Christian Coalition, who has called gambling "a cancer on the body politic, stealing food from the mouths of children, turning wives into widows." And Americans have historically viewed gambling as a temptation to be avoided. Their concern has usually not been over the immorality of gambling itself, but over the fact that gambling has often gone hand in hand with indolence, drinking, cheating, and sometimes violence. Until the 1970s, most states prohibited gambling, citing the evils associated with heavy gambling, such as bankruptcy and crime.

But gamblers who have been driven to poverty by their habit have more often been the objects of pity than condemnation. Those opposed to gambling tend to direct their moral outrage against the purveyors of gambling. Like tobacco companies, casinos are often attacked as irresponsible businesses that profit from their customers' addiction. State governments that hold lotteries have also received a heap of criticism: Antigambling activists argue that the government's role should be to discourage the vice of gambling, not promote it.

Public opinion polls indicate that the majority of Americans do not hold strong views on the morality of gambling. Many churches, for example, feel that raffles and bingo games are acceptable when the proceeds benefit charitable causes. Even people opposed to gambling tend to view it as imprudent or foolish rather than sinful. The authors in the following chapter offer their own views on whether gambling is immoral and whether government-sponsored lotteries are unethical.

"The idea that gambling is simple entertainment needs to be challenged."

Gambling Is Morally Questionable

Alberta Conference of Catholic Bishops

The Catholic bishops of Alberta, Canada, issued the following viewpoint after their 1998 conference. In it, they argue that although gambling is not expressly condemned by the Bible, many aspects of gambling are morally questionable. According to the bishops, gambling can be immoral if it harms others. This is often the case for heavy or compulsive gamblers, who may neglect their responsibilities to work or family because of their gambling. The authors also warn that gambling contradicts traditional Christian values: Rather than gambling, they argue, individuals should use their time and money to help the poor.

As you read, consider the following questions:

1. According to *The Catechism of the Catholic Church*, as quoted by the Catholic bishops of Alberta, when does gambling become morally unacceptable?
2. Approximately what percentage of gamblers will have problems controlling their gambling, according to the authors?
3. In the authors' opinion, what two guidelines should governments follow in order to maintain an ethical perspective on gambling?

The proliferation of government-sponsored gambling in our society has become a significant concern both for our Catholic community and our society. With government backing, the implication seems to be given that what is legal is therefore moral. Governments and other gambling proponents argue that gambling provides significant benefits to society.

Obviously, they point out, people wish to gamble. It has become a form of entertainment, often, even if not always, innocuous. In meeting this desire of many people, the government argues that it can best regulate the provision of gambling services, treating the income as a form of 'voluntary taxation.' Furthermore, besides providing jobs, the monies raised are almost always earmarked either for 'charitable causes' or general government expenses. And finally, if there are people who become addicted to gambling, then part of the proceeds can be put aside to treat the addiction problem.

This burgeoning fact of modern society deserves a commentary based on our Christian faith.

Traditionally, gambling has been looked upon with great suspicion in the Christian community. Marriages and families have been hurt or destroyed by compulsive gambling. The 'fantasy' motivation of entering the lap of luxury through winning is suspect. And the use of time and money in ways that hardly model Christian virtue and character suggest that the practice reflects neither Gospel values nor Christian inspiration.

Not a Black and White Issue

Nonetheless, the Catholic tradition has never simply condemned gambling as such. Our own history in Alberta provides ample evidence of the use of gambling to raise funds for everything from the construction of churches to charitable works. While most of this practice has been associated with the involvement of local communities in such things as raffles, bingos and draws, the presence and fact of gambling has not been lost in the public perception.

'Games of chance or wagers,' says *The Catechism of the Catholic Church* are not in themselves contrary to justice. 'They become morally unacceptable when they deprive someone of what is necessary to provide for his needs and those of others.' The Catechism, of course, does not address the more profound questions associated with an elaborate system of gambling.

Gambling Is Contrary to Christian Values

Exploiting the poor—Gambling preys on the desperation of the poor. . . . Scripture exhorts us to look out for the poor and disadvantaged, and issues strong warnings against taking advantage of their plight. . . .

Greed—Gambling is founded on greed and undergirded by a "get-rich-quick" appeal. . . . The Apostle Paul wrote in 1 Timothy 6:9–10a: "People who want to get rich fall into temptation and a trap and into many foolish and harmful desires that plunge men into ruin and destruction. For the love of money is a root of all kinds of evil.". . .

Covetousness—The 10th Commandment (Exodus 20:17) prohibits Christians from coveting another's possessions. Gambling is precisely the attempt to obtain the resources of others without providing anything of value in return. . . .

The role of government—The God-ordained purpose of government, as outlined in Romans 13:1–5, is to protect the welfare of the citizenry and to suppress evil. State-sanctioned gambling does the opposite. It victimizes many, especially the most vulnerable.

Ronald A. Reno, "Gambling and the Bible," Focus on the Family website, November 17, 1999, www.family.org/cforum/research/papers/a0008570.html.

Despite our history, there has also remained a deeper unease with compulsive gambling, ruinous gambling, and any gambling which detours the essentials of life, such as grocery money, away from their responsible use. This unease has at times in other Christian communities led to an understandable, complete moral condemnation of gambling in all forms.

Following our Catholic tradition, it seems important for the Bishops of Alberta to offer a more nuanced moral judgment of gambling and to issue a Gospel challenge to all Christians in the face of the increasing opportunities to gamble in our society.

The 'harmless' entertainment of gambling can simply be immoral if the necessities of family life are sacrificed. These necessities are not simply monetary. When gambling steals time and attention from spouse, children and family responsibilities, it is immoral.

Gambling, of course, can also become an addiction. While the mechanisms of who gets addicted are not always clearly understood, it is estimated that between three and five percent of gamblers will have a serious problem beyond their ability to control. A simplistic solution to this problem would be to suggest that anyone in danger of an addiction avoid gambling completely.

Since this problem usually surfaces after recreational gambling or at the end of long-term gambling, recognition and remedies must become more than the responsibility of the individual gambler. Programs to deal with the admitted gambler need to be complemented by efforts to identify and aid the compulsive gambler before disaster takes over.

An Ethical Response to Gambling

To associate all the evils of gambling with personal choice is to overlook the complicity of a system that needs gamblers in order to flourish. Thus, a major portion of an ethical response to gambling must come from a challenge to those who control the trade.

- First, problem gamblers need to be identified within the system and assisted before they 'hit bottom.'
- Second, those who are addicted need sufficient resources to help them.
- Third, those who commit crimes, especially theft, in order to feed a suddenly uncontrolled gambling habit should not be the only ones blamed for their crimes or be held solely responsible for restitution. When institutions are all-too-willing to take all the money a gambler throws away, ignoring the problems caused is not acceptable.
- Fourth, anything that contributes significantly to addictive forms of gambling—and video lottery terminals, which are proven to add the addictive power of television to that of gambling, must be mentioned here—should be banned or substantially altered in order to diminish the addictive power.
- Finally, if gambling is to be a personal choice, govern-

ments ought to restrict all promotion that serves to create a need as opposed to advertising services. One need only look at the glitter associated with gambling to recognize the temptation to make gambling a self-serving, 'growth' business.

Governments need an ethical perspective on their involvement in gambling.

First, studies ought to be done on where money that goes to gambling comes from; in other words, is this really disposable income or are such things as essential family needs or charitable donations or support for productive business being forfeited in favour of the easier, but less value-added dollar.

Second, as the major receivers of gambling monies, governments must take the responsibility for programs to aid addicts and to deter addictions. They also need to avoid seeing gambling as a cash cow to be milked for ever-increasing monies as pressure is liable to move gambling beyond entertainment.

If gambling is not to be decried as intrinsically evil, and if governments seem to think it is necessary to the economy, how should the Christian respond to this phenomenon? To begin with, a negative attitude of 'not doing anything wrong or harmful' is scarcely adequate as a Gospel-based response. Of course, the Christian should avoid misuse or abuse of funds for gambling. However, the idea that gambling is simple entertainment needs to be challenged as well, for the involvement is often not simple.

Gambling and Charity

An intrinsic part of the Christian tradition regards the monies available for gambling as the monies of the poor. That is to say, if those who gamble are wealthy enough to put money into games of chance, then a glance at Jesus' teaching in the Gospels suggests that they use the money to help the poor. The same could be said for much of the money and time most of us spend on various entertainments, so this is a meditation for all who have what is euphemistically referred to as 'disposable income.'

One might argue that the good causes to which wagered money is contributed fulfills this Christian challenge, as is often the case in local or community fund-raising events that use gambling. Many people do take advantage of such opportunities to donate to a good cause. However, when one participates in more serious 'gambling for entertainment,' it becomes important to examine one's motivations.

Donating to a good cause can often be completely lost track of in the thrill of gambling, in the escape from responsibility, in the almost anti-social atmosphere of commerce with a machine for hours. If there is money for gambling, perhaps we have simply not looked seriously enough at the gift of extra monies that God has given us to be used for good purposes. And if there is time for gambling, perhaps we need to look at whether we are allowing boredom to push us not into concern for others but the bright lights and action that will fill our hours for a price. The Christian challenge in the face of gambling is not to stop with a moral evaluation. Rather it is to look into the face and heart of Christ and see how Love motivates us to love our neighbour. Perhaps we cannot make this demand of governments, although if the poor are neglected because of gambling, then we must all raise our voices to demand at least a morally responsible control.

However, as Christians we can examine our own actions regarding gambling. And we can continue to look out for those who are harmed by gambling. And we can lobby that gambling is not allowed to harm communities and neighbourhoods. And we can preach and live the Word that ought to make gambling irrelevant in our lives. And we can live the hope of our faith that unmasks the false hope of greed.

> *"The popular perception—and the reality—*
> *[is] that gambling is just plain fun."*

Responsible Gambling Is Harmless Fun

Frank J. Fahrenkopf Jr.

Frank J. Fahrenkopf Jr. is president and chief executive officer of the American Gaming Association (AGA), a trade group representing the casino industry. In the following viewpoint, he argues that the vast majority of Americans view gambling as a fun and exciting form of entertainment. In Fahrenkopf's opinion, only a relatively small group of antigambling activists want the government to act as the "pleasure police" and restrict or prohibit gambling. Fahrenkopf acknowledges that a small proportion of gamblers are unable to control their gambling, but he argues that for most people gambling is simply an enjoyable way to spend their time and money, when done legally and responsibly.

As you read, consider the following questions:

1. What proportion of Americans had gambled in a casino in the past year, according to the survey cited by Fahrenkopf?
2. How does economics professor Robert McCormick describe gambling, as quoted by Fahrenkopf?
3. What is the Australian government's view of gambling, as quoted by the author?

"Who Wants to Be a Millionaire." "21." "Greed." It's no secret these new network television game shows are immensely popular. But why? According to some observers, they have achieved phenomenal success for the same reason casino gambling has taken off over the past two decades: Gambling is fun!

Ever since antiquity, people have engaged in some form of gambling. Dice have been recovered from Egyptian tombs, while the Chinese, Japanese, Greeks and Romans all were known to play games of skill and chance for amusement as early as 2300 B.C.

More recently, both Native Americans and European colonists had a history of gambling within their own cultures. Native Americans developed games of chance and believed that their gods determined fate and chance. British colonization of America was partly financed through lottery proceeds, beginning in the early 17th century, when lotteries were perceived as a popular voluntary form of taxation in Georgian England.

"Just Plain Fun"

Today, the popularity of gambling remains strong. One of two Americans played the lottery and more than a third gambled in a casino in the past year, according to a 2000 survey by national pollsters Peter Hart and Frank Luntz. The same survey found that more than 94 percent of Americans view casino gambling as a social activity, while 75 percent believe casino gambling can be a fun night out.

It may be that the entertainment value of gambling explains the popularity of "Who Wants to Be a Millionaire." According to a February Gallup poll, three of four Americans have watched "Millionaire." In analyzing the show's success, *Los Angeles Times* writer Paul Brownstein noted: "It's a form of recreational gambling, an intricate, hyperstylized casino game beamed into America's living rooms. And what it tells us is very true: Gambling is fun. A horribly self-destructive activity if it gets out of control, yes. But in the meantime fun. Fun, fun, fun."

Those sentiments were echoed by Robert McCormick, professor of economics at Clemson University. As he wrote in the *World and I*, "[Gamblers at American casinos] are middle America, and they are having fun. Biloxi, Las Vegas and Atlantic City are entertainment meccas. . . . Like spending hours watching TV or an evening listening to Porgy and Bess, it is just plain fun."

Public Acceptance of Gambling

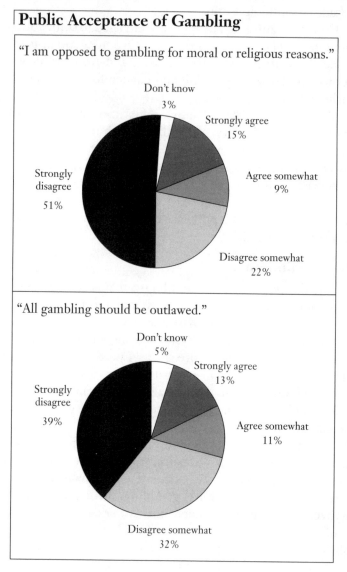

"I am opposed to gambling for moral or religious reasons."

Don't know 3%
Strongly agree 15%
Agree somewhat 9%
Disagree somewhat 22%
Strongly disagree 51%

"All gambling should be outlawed."

Don't know 5%
Strongly agree 13%
Agree somewhat 11%
Disagree somewhat 32%
Strongly disagree 39%

Don Feeney, "Is Gambling Immoral?" *Beyond the Odds*, June 1999, www.miph.org/gambling/bto/jun99/1.html.

As we defend our industry, sometimes we forget to remind people that beyond the important jobs we provide, the economic development we generate and the capital investment we make in our communities, there's another important element that's critical to our success: our customers enjoy the entertainment experience we provide.

And yet we often are faced with attacks from opponents who can't see that reality. While a small number of people don't gamble responsibly and deserve our attention, the overwhelming majority does. Many of us have friends who gather in Las Vegas every year for the Super Bowl or March Madness. Or we know of war veterans and old friends who have met there for a reunion. And we certainly recognize that hundreds of thousands of conventioneers have designated Las Vegas as their preferred destination. Even the Southern Baptists have met in Las Vegas. Why? Because it's fun. They come to our resorts to see a concert or a show, shop, dine at one of our fine restaurants, and, yes, to gamble. As Gerri Hirshey wrote in the *New York Times Magazine*: "You do see it all here in the Gambling Nation, people of different races, incomes, playing skills and ages having a swell time rump to rump."

The Antigambling Minority

Few people want to see the federal government take on the role of "pleasure police," yet that is precisely what opponents of our business have been asking them to do. U.S. Representative Barney Frank (D-Mass.) recently criticized those who would attempt to limit senior citizens' rights to make their own decisions, specifically in regard to gambling. "To me, this is one more instance of the Dumbing Down of Senior Citizens," Representative Frank said in the June 6, 2000, Congressional Record. "Are older people perceived to be so witless, so gullible, that we need to be protected from ourselves lest we buy too many lottery tickets or play Bingo too often? Do we need Big Brother to watch over us at the blackjack tables and slot machines? . . . I defend the right of anyone over age 21 to spend their money where they please—be it a casino bingo hall, sports arena, vacation resort, etc."

Some governments have publicly recognized the entertainment value of gambling. The Australian government, for example, recently conceded that point in its federal review of gambling: "The benefits of liberalisation of the gambling industries come primarily from the satisfaction that consumers obtain from the ability to access what for many is a desired form of entertainment."

Despite the popular perception—and the reality—that gambling is just plain fun, it appears that gambling will remain under siege by the small but vocal opposition that would like to see its elimination as a legal form of entertainment. But Guy Calvert, a mathematician and quantitative analyst at a Wall Street firm, argues in the *World and I* that the regulatory experiences of the past should be a reliable guide in determining future gambling policy. "Historically . . . gambling prohibitions have done more harm than good. [W]e recognize that alcoholism is best addressed on a voluntary basis rather than through outlawing drinking. Likewise, the best recourse for compulsive gamblers may be counseling and abstinence, not government intervention to prohibit or otherwise limit gambling."

While the busybodies of the world continue their fight, we, too, will continue to defend the rights of our customers who enjoy the entertainment options we offer. We're accustomed to being in the hot seat. But with 28 million "Millionaire" viewers every night it's on and 75 million-plus casino visitors every year, it's clear that most people agree that gambling is fun.

And that's my final answer.

"It's not the place of government to encourage people to gamble."

State Lotteries Are an Unethical Source of Government Revenue

Michael Nelson

In the following viewpoint, Michael Nelson argues that state governments should not use lotteries as means of generating nontax revenues. According to Nelson, lotteries are extremely regressive, since poor people purchase the majority of lottery tickets. Furthermore, he argues, state governments quickly become dependent on lottery revenues, and begin advertising programs to encourage more people to play the lottery. In Nelson's opinion, these campaigns are unethical because they encourage gambling and thus discourage hard work, saving, and investment. Michael Nelson is a professor of political science at Rhodes College in Memphis, Tennessee, and the coauthor of *Governing Gambling: Politics and Policy in State, Tribe, and Nation*.

As you read, consider the following questions:
1. What percent of the nation's population lives in states with lotteries, according to the author?
2. What statistics does the author offer to emphasize the problem of minors betting on the lottery?
3. In Nelson's view, what reasons do liberals and conservatives each give for opposing lotteries?

Here's the best news to come out of the otherwise screwed-up 2000 election: The political juggernaut that during the last third of the twentieth century transformed the states from staunch foes of gambling into gambling's chief sponsors has slowed to a crawl. The voters of Arkansas rejected a lottery-casino ballot measure, joining the voters of Alabama, who turned down a lottery proposal in 1999. South Carolina voters were more ambivalent: They approved a lottery proposal, but they also elected a Republican House of Representatives that may refuse to pass the enabling legislation needed to put a lottery into effect.

The Spread of Lotteries

What a contrast to the period that began in 1964, when New Hampshire became the first state ever to create, own, and operate a lottery. New Hampshire is one of only two states with neither an income tax nor a sales tax, and therein lies the tale. A lottery seemed to the state's voters a painless, voluntary tax.

Lotteries spread rapidly in this country during the 1970s and 1980s, when New Hampshire seemed a model to many states. In 1978 California voters passed Proposition 13, which placed severe restrictions on the state's taxing authority and inspired voters in some other states to enact similar measures. More important, Prop 13 and its progeny made politicians everywhere averse to new taxes. Only one state, Connecticut, has enacted a personal income tax or general sales tax since 1977. Ronald Reagan was elected president in 1980 on a promise to make substantial reductions in federal income tax rates. He not only accomplished this goal but also persuaded Congress to reduce spending on grant programs to the states.

To state governments caught in a vise between greater revenue needs and widespread opposition to taxes, the lottery seemed an appealing way out. During the late 1960s and the 1970s, 12 states (mostly in the Northeast) legalized lotteries. During the 1980s, 18 states—representing a majority of every region of the country except the South—followed suit. Six more states, including three in the South, legalized lotteries in the early 1990s. In all, 37 state governments and the District of Columbia—representing nearly 90 percent of the nation's population—now own and operate lotteries.

The desire for nontax revenues was not the only thing fueling the spread of lotteries; there also was competitive pressure on the states that didn't have a lottery. Once a critical mass of lottery states was reached, a race to the bottom began. In 1986, for example, John Carlin, the liberal Democratic governor of Kansas and an opponent of lotteries, saw how many dollars were flowing out of his state as people crossed the border to play in Missouri and Colorado. Carlin became a lottery convert, arguing that "not having one when your neighbor has one is like tying one hand behind your back." Kansas's story was repeated nearly everywhere. As the political scientists Frances Stokes Berry and William Berry found, the greater the number of lottery states that border a state without one, the more likely that state is to adopt a lottery.

A Deal with the Devil

What a deal with the devil Carlin and his fellow governors struck. To begin with, lotteries are a wildly regressive way of raising revenue. Although members of nearly every demographic group bet the lottery in roughly equal numbers, some bet much more frequently than others did. "The heaviest players," Duke University economists Charles Clotfelter and Philip Cook have found, are "blacks, high-school dropouts, and people in the lowest income category." Yet state lotteries depend on the participation of these frequent players. "If all players spent the same as the median player, $75 a year" report Clotfelter and Cook, "[lottery ticket] sales would fall by 76 percent." Eighty-two percent of lottery bets are made by just 20 percent of players—and this group is disproportionately poor, black, and uneducated.

Despite laws to the contrary, minors bet the lottery, too. The presence of lottery tickets alongside candy, chips, and crackers in neighborhood convenience stores places children directly in contact with gambling. In lottery states, three-fourths of high school seniors report having bet in a lottery, according to the 1999 report of the National Gambling Impact Study Commission. In Massachusetts the attorney general found that children as young as age nine were able to buy lottery tickets in 80 percent of their attempts.

An additional problem with lotteries is that the money that states make from them seldom goes where the law says it should. Eighteen states earmark their lottery revenues for education; others, for transportation or programs for seniors. But economists have discovered that in most states little if any net increase in spending for the earmarked purpose actually occurs. Instead these states substitute lottery revenues for money they otherwise would have spent from their general funds.

Government Promotion of Vice

Perhaps the worst thing about lotteries is that they put states into the business of gambling, which generates its own downward spiral of increasing regressivity and deception. States come to depend on the revenues from lottery games as part of their ongoing budgets. But people get bored betting the same games over and over again. Ticket sales and revenues to the state treasury drop. So state lottery agencies ramp up their advertising, much of which is designed to persuade those who already bet a great deal to bet a great deal more.

The federal government is no help. Although commercial sweepstakes operators like Publishers Clearinghouse are governed by the Federal Trade Commission's truth-in-advertising rules, Congress has exempted state lotteries from such restraints. With few exceptions, lottery agencies use their freedom from federal regulation to advertise their games misleadingly, thereby fostering the impression that the odds of winning a big prize are good and that playing the lottery is a sensible way to enhance one's financial status. In doing so, these agencies encourage luck—not hard work or saving and investment—as a strategy for success.

"When I was younger, I suppose I could have done more to plan my future" says a smiling young man in a commercial for the Connecticut lottery. "But I didn't. Or I could have made some smart investments. But I didn't. Heck, I could have bought a one-dollar Connecticut lotto ticket, won a jackpot worth millions, and gotten a nice big check every year for 20 years. And I did! I won!" The commercial ends with a voice-over saying, "Overall chance of winning is one in 30." But that is the chance of winning a small prize in an instant lottery, not "a jackpot worth millions."

Bettors may become less and less susceptible to commercials like this, but they are hardly immune to the epidemic at large. State lottery agencies, pressured by their governors and legislatures to keep the revenues coming, develop new, more enticing games. Over the years, the monthly drawing has given way to the daily drawing, the instant scratch-off game, and lotto. The five states that have recently decided to market slot machine–style video lottery terminals may represent the wave of the future. In the late 1990s, lottery revenues fell in nearly half the states; but the video states experienced annual growth rates ranging from 9 percent to 26 percent.

Until recently political conditions seemed ripe for a new round of state lottery enactments. Except for Alaskans and Hawaiians, every American lives in a state that either has a lottery or shares a border with one or more lottery states. Ambitious politicians in non-lottery states have a strong incentive to urge such enactments. Lotteries are a normal activity of state government, they argue, pointing to the money the state loses when its people cross the border to bet in other states.

Lotteries on the Decline?

But the rejection of a lottery by the voters of Alabama and Arkansas, as well as South Carolinians' tepid approval of one, suggests that the political tide may have turned. Before 1999 referenda to create state-run lotteries were almost unbeatable: 32 passed, and only two (both in North Dakota) were defeated. Since 1999 lottery referenda have gone one for three. Voters in Maine, a lottery state since 1974, turned down a ballot measure in the 2000 election to allow video gambling at racetracks. Tennessee voters are far from certain to approve a lottery in 2002, when a referendum is scheduled to take place. That's a big change from just a few years ago, when easy passage would have been a sure thing.

Lotteries are on the political decline for several reasons. The recently formed National Coalition Against Legalized Gambling (NCALG), a grass-roots organization that can be counted on to set up shop in almost any state that is considering a lottery, deserves part of the credit. NCALG is especially good at rousing opponents from both ends of the political spectrum. Liberals are called to arms by the issues of social justice that a lottery raises. Conservatives are energized by their conviction that gambling is morally destructive.

Anyway, the promise of new revenues from a lottery is less alluring than it used to be. Now that lotteries have been around long enough for economists and other social scientists to study their effects, the word is out: They're bad news. They are regressive, deceptive, and—for both children and adults—enticing to the point of being addictive. The revenues they generate for a state are roughly equivalent to those that an increase in the sales tax of less than 1 percent would produce. But the main argument against lotteries should have been as apparent to New Hampshire 37 years ago as it is to Alabama and Arkansas today: It's not the place of government to encourage people to gamble.

> *"Unlike taxes, lottery purchases are both voluntary and overwhelmingly preferred by the public."*

State Lotteries Are an Ethical Source of Government Revenue

North American Association of State and
Provincial Lotteries

The North American Association of State and Provincial Lotteries (NASPL) represents forty-six lottery organizations throughout North America. The organization works to inform the public about the benefits of lotteries. In the following viewpoint, the NASPL answers several frequently asked questions about lotteries. The NASPL disputes common claims that lotteries are played mostly by poor or uneducated people. The organization also denies that lottery advertising is misleading or directed at lower-income groups. Lotteries have raised billions of dollars for state and provincial governments, the authors point out, much of which has been used to fund education, health care, and other worthy causes.

As you read, consider the following questions:
1. On average, what proportion of state and provincial budgets do lottery revenues account for, according to the authors?
2. What is the "pareto principle," as defined by the authors?
3. What explanation does the NASPL offer for why the odds of winning do not appear on all lottery advertisements?

Excerpted from "Frequently Asked Questions," by the North American Association of State and Provincial Lotteries, www.naspl.org. Copyright © 2000 by the North American Association of State and Provincial Lotteries. Reprinted with permission.

*H*ow many lotteries are there? In North America every Canadian province, 38 U.S. states, the District of Columbia, Puerto Rico, and the U.S. Virgin Islands all offer government-operated lotteries. Elsewhere in the world publicly-operated lotteries exist in at least 100 countries on every inhabited continent. In some cases they are operated by national governments, in other cases by state or provincial governments, and in still others by cities. . . .

Lottery Revenues

What do lottery revenues benefit? Lottery proceeds benefit different programs in different jurisdictions. In many cases lottery profits are combined with tax and other revenues in a government's general fund. In other cases lottery proceeds are dedicated to a wide range of causes, including education, economic development, the environment, programs for senior citizens, health care, sports facilities, capital construction projects, cultural activities, tax relief, and others.

Who decides where the money goes? In a few cases the recipients of lottery proceeds are specified in a jurisdiction's constitution, but in most cases this decision is up to that state or province's elected officials. . . .

How much money do lotteries raise? Since the New Hampshire lottery was founded in 1964, lotteries have raised over $150 billion for government programs in North America. In fiscal year '00 Canadian lotteries transferred $2.7 billion ($CAN) to their beneficiaries, while U.S. lotteries turned over $12 billion ($US) to theirs.

Aren't lotteries an inefficient way to raise revenue? Certainly lotteries are more expensive to administer than taxes, assuming we consider only the cost to government and not the costs to businesses and individuals in complying with tax laws. However, unlike taxes, lottery purchases are both voluntary and overwhelmingly preferred by the public.

But doesn't the government risk becoming "addicted" to lottery profits? On the average, lotteries account for one-half of one percent of their state or provincial budgets. Governments are far, far, more dependent on tax and fee revenues than they are lottery proceeds. Voluntary, non-tax revenue sources are obviously more popular than taxes, and always will be.

Purchasing Lottery Tickets

Where are lottery tickets sold? Lottery tickets are sold at more than 240,000 locations throughout North America. Most of these locations are conventional retail outlets such as convenience stores, gas stations, and supermarkets. . . .

Isn't it true that lotteries deliberately place more ticket outlets in low-income neighborhoods? No. Lotteries place their ticket outlets where there are qualifying stores. In many cases zoning regulations in upper-income communities mean that these communities have few or no gas stations or supermarkets, and hence few or no lottery retailers. City neighborhoods, by contrast, often have many qualifying retailers because of the population density in these areas and hence many lottery outlets. In addition, many "low-income" areas (such as downtown areas) are, in fact, commercial or industrial centers with a large influx of higher-income people during the workday.

But shouldn't the lotteries restrict the sale of tickets in low-income areas? To deny a government contract to a retailer who meets basic financial and integrity standards would be very difficult. Such restrictions are clearly discriminatory against retailers located in these neighborhoods and would likely face a serious legal challenge. . . .

Who Plays Lotteries?

Who buys lottery tickets? I understand it's mostly poor people. A recent Gallup Poll on Gambling in America found that 57% of American adults reported buying a lottery ticket in the past 12 months. People with incomes of $45,000 to $75,000 were the most likely to play—65 percent had played in the past year—while those with incomes under $25,000 were the least likely to play at 53 percent. Further, people with incomes in excess of $75,000 spend roughly three times as much on lotteries each month as do those with incomes under $25,000.

In addition, surveys of gambling behavior have been conducted in a number of jurisdictions. In Colorado, for example, people with annual incomes of $15,000 or less make up 7 percent of the population but only 5 percent of those playing the lottery in the past 30 days. In Georgia, an Atlanta

Journal and Constitution Survey found that only 8.6 percent of lottery players had incomes of $24,000 or less, while 27 percent had incomes between $50,000 and $74,000. In addition, 33 percent were high school graduates, 22 percent had some college, 25 percent had a college degree, and 10 percent had an advanced degree. A 1998 Texas study found that those with less than a high school education and those with the lowest incomes were least likely to play. And in Minnesota a 1998 study found that the 13 percent of the population with incomes under $20,000 made up only 9 percent of the past year's ticket buyers while those with incomes higher than $50,000 were disproportionately more likely to play.

But not all of these people play the same amount. Don't most lottery sales come from a relatively small number of people? As with any product or service, some people are more enthusiastic consumers than others. Business schools teach marketing students the "pareto principle": the idea that no matter what the product, 80 percent of the sales will come from 20 percent of the customers. Lotteries are no different. A Minnesota study, for example, found that 20 percent of the lottery players account for 71 percent of lottery income. In Arizona, 24 percent of lottery players accounted for 70 percent of lottery spending, and in Pennsylvania 29 percent of the players accounted for 79 percent of the spending on the lottery.

What about the heaviest lottery players? Aren't they poor, undereducated, and desperate? Again, no. Numerous studies conducted in a wide range of jurisdictions show that frequent or "heavy" lottery players closely resemble the overall population of that state or province. They are no more likely to be poor or have little formal education than a citizen selected at random. . . .

Don't poor people spend a higher percentage of their incomes on lottery tickets than those of greater means? Poor people spend a larger proportion of their income than wealthy people on any item having a fixed price and general appeal. Poor people pay proportionately more for food, medicine, clothing, utilities, insurance, and housing, as well as for payroll and sales taxes. People who are well-off, on the other hand, spend a higher percentage of their income on things that the poor cannot afford, such as overseas vacations or season tickets to cultural or sporting events. The rich also invest and gamble in stock and commodity markets—also activities the poor cannot afford.

Lotteries Benefit the Public

Gambling is a voluntary activity. Nobody is forced to enter a casino or pick up a playing card. If you disapprove, don't do it. . . .

But the [National Gambling Impact Study Commission] took a poke at state lotteries, on the grounds that government services should not be financed largely on the backs of the low-income minorities and other poor people who are the heaviest players. The commission urged states and communities to consider a moratorium on new lotteries until the social consequences can be further evaluated.

Fiddlesticks. That is bleeding-heart liberalism at its bloodiest. Lotteries are a clean way to get people to do voluntarily what they resent doing through mandatory taxes, which is to pay for education and other public necessities. If lotteries offer impossible hope against insurmountable odds, so be it. A buck is a cheap price to pay for a dream, however temporary.

Marianne Means, *Seattle Post-Intelligencer*, July 7, 1999.

Lottery opponents have pointed out, though, that unlike spending on, say, a movie ticket, the lottery ticket is purchased from the government and is therefore a regressive tax. But the lottery is not a tax. Webster defines a tax as "a compulsory payment . . . for the support of government." No one is coerced to play the lottery. The purchase of a lottery ticket is completely voluntary—and a lot more fun than filling out Form 1040.

Ultimately, though, the important question isn't the percentage of income spent. It's whether the less affluent are spending an unduly large portion of their income on lottery tickets. This has undoubtedly happened in some instances just as it undoubtedly happened with junk food, athletic shoes, and other consumer items. However, there is no evidence suggesting that it is anything approaching the norm. The overwhelming majority of poor people, along with the overwhelming majority of upper-income people, play with restraint and moderation.

But shouldn't the government try to keep those who can least afford it from spending their money on the lottery? This question implies that economically disadvantaged people are somehow less capable of making a decision on how to spend a dollar than those of greater means or that they are not entitled to the same opportunities for entertainment and recreation than the rest of us. The poor are allowed to vote, get married, and sign contracts. Society in the U.S. and Canada does not usurp rights and privileges based on socioeconomic status. The poor have to budget and watch their expenditures much more carefully than the rich. Economic status is not a measure of intelligence.

Lottery Advertising

How much do lotteries advertise? In 1996 North American lotteries spent $400 million ($US) on advertising and received $34 billion in sales. Advertising expenditures accounted for 1.17 percent of total revenue. By contrast, restaurant owners spent 3.2 percent of their revenues on advertising, beverage manufacturers 7.5 percent, cosmetics companies 8.8 percent, and candy makers 12.7 percent. Advertising accounts for less of the cost of a lottery ticket than virtually any other consumer product.

Why can lotteries advertise when casinos can't? Casinos can, and do, advertise. A recent Supreme Court decision cleared the way for casinos to advertise throughout the country. But even before this decision, casino advertising was extensive. According to the recent Saul F. Leonard Company's Study of U.S. Gaming, the MGM Grand casino alone spent $51,622,000 on advertising and promotion in 1994.

Lottery advertising isn't regulated by the Federal Trade Commission. Why not? Lotteries are not subject to FTC regulation because they are operated by state governments, and the federal government cannot regulate state government programs. Unlike other products, however, lottery advertising is subject to review and restriction by governors and state and provincial legislators. . . .

Is lottery advertising targeted to the poor? No. This would be both a bad business decision and a bad political decision. It's a bad business decision to target marketing to a small portion of the population with the least disposable income and who are the least likely to buy the product. It's a bad political decision as such a practice is almost certain to earn a lottery the wrath of the governor, the legislature, and the media. . . .

Why aren't the odds of winning all lottery prizes on all ads? Why aren't all food ingredients listed on all ads? Because of the limited time and space available on advertisements and the likelihood that they would have to be either spoken too fast or appear in too small print to be easily comprehended. All lotteries make the odds of winning available in print at the point of sale, often on the ticket itself, much as food ingredients are available at the store on the product label.

Lotteries and Compulsive Gambling

Do lotteries contribute to compulsive gambling? There are certainly pathological and problem gamblers who play the lottery to excess. They are, however, few and far between. According to the Iowa Department of Human Services after 10 years of the lottery's existence only 6 percent of the calls to the state's problem gambling hotline related to lottery play. In Minnesota, it was 4 percent in 1997. Also in Minnesota, of the 944 admitted to the state's gambling treatment centers from 1990 to 1996, only eight cited the lottery as their preferred game. A Colorado study found that problem gamblers were 4.7 times more likely to have visited a casino in the past week and 5.2 times more likely to have played bingo than non-problem gamblers. By contrast, they were only 1.9 times more likely to have played the lottery, the lowest figure of any form of gambling. An Iowa State University study found that having more than one marriage, frequently changing residences, being a member of a minority group, and serving in the armed forces had higher correlations with problem gambling than did playing the lottery.

Most conclusively, the recent National Survey on Gambling Behavior conducted for the National Gambling Impact Study Commission found that "it does not appear that the availability of a lottery has an impact on (problem gambling) prevalence rates." In fact, they found that problem gamblers were only slightly more likely to be lottery players than were members of the general public. By contrast, they were more than five times as likely to have made an "unlicensed" (often illegal) wager and more than four times as likely to have visited a racetrack. . . .

Lottery Regulation

Can state governments be trusted to regulate lotteries when they benefit from the lottery proceeds? State regulatory proceedings are much more open and accessible to the public than the workings of federal regulatory agencies. All lottery board meetings are public, as are all legislative hearings. Lottery files are public records, subject at any time to media scrutiny. Lottery opponents in a legislature can examine the smallest lottery details and vote on lottery business operations. (In what other business would those opposed to the business' existence be permitted a vote on business operations?) And if the public does not approve of the way a lottery is run, they have recourse to the ballot box and the ultimate sanction of refusing to buy tickets. Those who claim that lotteries are not regulated are really complaining that the regulators have made decisions they don't agree with.

If the states cannot be trusted to regulate lotteries because they make a relatively small amount of money on them (an average of ½ of 1 percent of the state budget) it follows that they should not be allowed to make their own tax policy as well.

Can't lotteries be privatized? Yes, they could be. Certainly many of the day-to-day activities of lotteries are done under contract or are privatized, and the retailers selling lottery tickets are almost all private businesses. However, the public has a right to demand both the security and integrity of lotteries, to ensure that everyone stands an equal chance of winning, that all advertised prizes are in fact paid out, and that the lottery does not resort to unscrupulous business practices. It is true that these factors also apply to casinos, but it is much easier to police operations at a handful of casinos than at thousands of lottery retail outlets. Remember that lotteries were abolished in the 1800s because of the dishonesty of private operators.

But at least with a private lottery the government would not be sponsoring an activity I consider to be immoral. There are many government activities that some consider to be immoral, ranging from defense spending to the teaching of evolution. Citizens do not have the option of paying taxes only to support those programs they approve of. By contrast no one is forced to buy a lottery ticket.

Lottery Odds

Is it true that the odds of winning the lottery are worse than being struck by lightning? No, even if we just consider the awarding of large jackpots. In 1996 1,136 people won $1,000,000 or more playing North American lotteries. An additional 4,520 won $100,000 or more. By contrast, 91 people were killed by lightning.

In addition, there's no second prize in a lightning strike. In a lottery, you win lesser amounts of money by coming close to the winning numbers. On many games odds of 1 in 5 or 1 in 4 are not uncommon. Lotteries award over $50 million in prizes in North America every day. Lightning isn't nearly that productive.

Periodical Bibliography

The following articles have been selected to supplement the diverse views presented in this chapter. Addresses are provided for periodicals not indexed in the *Readers' Guide to Periodical Literature*, the *Alternative Press Index*, the *Social Sciences Index*, or the *Index to Legal Periodicals and Books*.

Christianity Today	"Fortuna's Rule," November 11, 1998.
Robert R. Detlefsen	"Wagers of Sin," *Reason*, December 1997.
John J. Egan	"State-Sanctioned Gambling Is a Bad Bet," *U.S. Catholic*, November 1997.
William A. Glaston and David Wasserman	"Gambling Away Our Moral Capital," *Public Interest*, Spring 1996.
Clyde Haberman	"Lottery Fever: States Feed It, and Catch It," *New York Times*, July 31, 1998.
Blake Hurst	"The Government as Gambling Partner," *American Enterprise*, March/April 1996.
Richard C. Leone and Bernard Wasow	"The Savings Lottery: A Dollar and a Dream," *American Prospect*, January 3, 2000.
Richard McGowan	"Games of Chance Promote Valuable Causes Worldwide," *Forum for Applied Research and Public Policy*, Summer 1996.
Richard McGowan	"Lotteries and Sin Taxes: Painless Revenue or Painful Mirage?" *America*, April 30, 1994.
National Review	"The House Wins," September 1, 1998.
Michael Nelson	"Morality, Politics, and Gambling," *Vital Speeches of the Day*, April 15, 2000.
Michael J. Sandel	"Bad Bet," *New Republic*, March 10, 1997.
Daniel Seligman	"Why I Gamble," *National Review*, May 1, 1995.
Joshua Wolf Shenk	"Everyone's a Loser," *Washington Monthly*, July/August 1995.
Tim Stafford	"None Dare Call It a Sin," *Christianity Today*, May 18, 1998.

How Serious Is the Problem of Compulsive Gambling?

Chapter Preface

"Others may get their rush from drugs and alcohol, but my high comes from gambling," writes "Denise" in the October 1999 issue of *Essence* magazine. In the article she relates her lifelong passion for gambling, and how this passion slowly turned into addiction. Growing up she often played poker with family and friends; after she turned twenty-one, she began making monthly trips to Atlantic City and thrice-weekly trips to Soaring Eagle, a Native American casino three hours away from her hometown of Detroit.

In 1994, a casino opened in Windsor, Ontario, a less than half-hour drive for Denise. She filed for bankruptcy in 1995.

Ironically, Denise works as a psychiatric social worker, helping people with addictions, but only after she hit near-bottom was she able to spot her own problem. After filing for bankruptcy, Denise enrolled in a 12-Step program for compulsive gamblers. This support group helped Denise avoid casinos for a few months, but she eventually relapsed, and truly hit bottom. She began gambling more than ever. She stayed at the casino until very late at night, and it began affecting her job performance. Once, after a quarrel with her supervisor, she stalked out of work and headed straight for the casino. By this time she had sold almost everything she owned and was $80,000 in debt. When she finally came home that night she made a desperate suicide attempt, which fortunately failed.

Denise has been in recovery since that horrible night. She began attending support meetings again, and now works as a psychotherapist specializing in compulsive gambling. When counseling other problem gamblers, she tells them what experience has taught her: "I've learned that gambling is no friend of mine. It may be fun for some people, but for me it can be deadly."

Denise's story shows in dramatic detail how compulsive gambling can take over a person's life. In the following chapter, the authors debate the severity and prevalence of this disorder.

"[Problem gambling is] an addictive illness in which the subject is driven by an overwhelming, uncontrollable impulse to gamble."

Compulsive Gambling Is an Addiction

Ronald M. Pavalko

In the following viewpoint, Ronald M. Pavalko argues that problem gambling (a broad term that includes compulsive gambling) is a "hidden addiction" that afflicts millions of Americans. Problem gamblers, he argues, are addicted to gambling in much the same way that alcoholics or drug addicts are addicted to drinking and using drugs. Rather than being dependent on a substance, he explains, problem gamblers are addicted to the emotional thrill of gambling. Pavalko is emeritus professor of sociology at the University of Wisconsin-Parkside in Kenosha, Wisconsin, and director of the university's Center for Gambling Studies. He is a member of the National Council on Problem Gambling and the author of *Risky Business: America's Fascination with Gambling*.

As you read, consider the following questions:

1. In the author's view, what is the most important thing that distinguishes compulsive gamblers from recreational gamblers?
2. What are two of the reasons Pavalko offers to explain why problem gambling is a "hidden addiction"?

Excerpted from "Problem Gambling: The Hidden Addiction," by Ronald M. Pavalko, *National Forum: The Phi Kappa Phi Journal*, vol. 79, no. 4, Fall 1999. Copyright © 1999 by Ronald M. Pavalko. Reprinted by permission of the publishers.

Problem gambling has received a great deal of attention recently. In June 1999 the Congressionally mandated National Gambling Impact Study Commission (NGISC) completed two years of deliberations and issued a report calling, among other things, for greater attention to problem gambling from the states (especially those operating lotteries and licensing and taxing casinos and race tracks). The gambling industry, especially the casino segment, has acknowledged that problem gambling is a by-product of gambling expansion and has begun promoting "responsible gaming." National television network programs dealing with problem gamblers and their families also have increased in frequency. Despite all this, problem gambling remains very much a "hidden addiction," despite the fact that it is every bit as real as an addiction to alcohol or other drugs.

The main concern of this viewpoint is identifying some of the reasons why problem gambling is a hidden or unrecognized addiction. But first, it is essential to explain what problem gambling is and just how prevalent it is. In doing so, we find that some of the factors contributing to the hidden nature of this addiction should become apparent.

A Terminological Caveat

Unfortunately, the terms "pathological," "compulsive," "disordered," and "problem" gambling are often used interchangeably to describe this addiction. Strictly speaking, pathological/compulsive/disordered gambling refers to gambling that meets at least five of the American Psychiatric Association's ten criteria for pathological gambling. (These criteria are presented in Table 1.) *DSM* refers to the American Psychiatric Association's *Diagnostic and Statistical Manual*, and "*IV*" simply refers to the fourth edition of the Manual.

The term "problem gambling" is often used in two different ways. It is used to refer to gambling in which people develop family, work, or financial problems as a result of their gambling but do not exhibit the extreme characteristics of pathological gambling. It also is used in a more inclusive way to capture both pathological/compulsive/disordered gambling at one extreme and any involvement with gambling that creates problems in people's lives at the other extreme.

The distinction is similar to what we find in the area of alcoholism. Not all problem drinkers are alcoholics, but alcoholics certainly have a drinking problem.

Table 1

The American Psychiatric Association's Diagnostic Criteria for Pathological Gambling (*DSM-IV*)

1. Preoccupied with gambling (preoccupied with reliving past gambling experiences, handicapping, or planning the next venture, or thinking of ways to get money with which to gamble).

2. Needs to gamble with increasing amounts of money in order to achieve the desired excitement.

3. Restlessness or irritability when attempting to cut down or stop gambling.

4. Gambles as a way of escaping from problems or relieving dysphoric mood (feelings of helplessness, guilt, anxiety, or depression).

5. After losing money gambling, often returns another day in order to get even ("chasing" one's losses).

6. Lies to family members or others to conceal the extent of involvement with gambling.

7. Illegal acts (forgery, fraud, theft, embezzlement) are committed in order to finance gambling.

8. Has jeopardized or lost significant relationship, job, or educational or career opportunity because of gambling.

9. Reliance on others to provide money to relieve a desperate financial situation caused by gambling (a bailout).

10. Repeated unsuccessful efforts to control, cut back, or stop gambling.

American Psychiatric Association, *Diagnostic and Statistical Manual of Mental Disorders, Fourth Edition.* Washington, DC: American Psychiatric Association, 1994.

What these terminology differences mean is that there is a range or continuum of difficulties that some people get into with gambling. My own preference is to use the term "problem gambling" in the more inclusive way, and I will do so here except when quoting or referring to writing that uses other terms.

For the overwhelming majority of people who gamble, it

is a harmless recreational and leisure time activity. However, for some, gambling is a totally different experience.

The serious study of problem gambling is a relatively recent phenomenon. Since the early 1970s, research and clinical experience have come together to produce a fairly clear picture of problem gambling that fits an "illness model." Problem gambling has become "medicalized" in the sense that it is seen as a disease which is essentially an addiction. One of the pioneers in the study of problem gambling, psychiatrist Robert Custer, defined it as "an addictive illness in which the subject is driven by an overwhelming, uncontrollable impulse to gamble. The impulse progresses in intensity and urgency, consuming more and more of the individual's time, energy, and emotional and material resources. Ultimately, it invades, undermines, and often destroys everything that is meaningful in his life." Although no substance is involved, this could substitute for a definition of alcohol and other drug addiction. Others [such as researchers Richard J. Rosenthal and Henry R. Lesieur] have described it as "a progressive disorder characterized by a continuous or periodic loss of control over gambling; a preoccupation with gambling and with obtaining money with which to gamble; irrational thinking; and a continuation of the behavior despite adverse consequences." This, too, is fundamentally a definition of an addiction.

Problem gamblers have an intense preoccupation with gambling. Their lives are focused on gambling, to the exclusion of other interests. They gamble more often and with more money than they intend, and they have great difficulty controlling the amount of money they wager or the amount of time they spend gambling.

Like people addicted to drugs, problem gamblers develop tolerance. They need to increase the amount of money wagered in order to achieve the desired excitement. They escalate from simple to "exotic" wagers, where both the risks and the potential winnings are great.

Problem gamblers also experience withdrawal symptoms when they attempt to cut back or stop their gambling. When they cannot get to a gambling venue, or when they do not have money with which to gamble, problem gamblers may get irritable, nervous, and restless. Perhaps the most important thing that distinguishes problem gamblers from recreational gamblers is chasing. When they lose, compulsive gamblers chase their losses in an attempt to get even or win back what they have lost. When they lose, most recreational gamblers walk away from their losses without further consequences. Problem gamblers cannot do that. They make every effort to return as soon as they can (that is, as soon as they can get more money) to try to win back what they have lost.

Problem gamblers try to keep their gambling, and especially their losses and debts, a secret as long as possible. They construct elaborate lies to conceal their activities and related problems. A big part of this is lying to family and friends about their gambling activities, their losses, and their debts.

When their financial difficulties become severe, problem gamblers may engage in illegal activities to obtain money with which to gamble or to pay off gambling debts. Their debts create a situation where they constantly need money to pay off loans and continue gambling. In studies of 394 members of Gamblers Anonymous in Illinois, Wisconsin, and Connecticut, 57 percent admitted to stealing in various ways to finance their gambling. The total amount of money stolen was $30,065,812 for an average of $76,309. Committing crimes is often a matter of convenience, opportunity, or the ease with which money can be obtained. An employer's funds or a client's account are seen by the problem gambler as an easy solution to his or her problems. The most common crimes committed by problem gamblers are embezzlement, forgery, misappropriation of funds, and tax and insurance fraud. "White collar" crimes predominate, but robbery, burglary, shoplifting, and drug dealing also occur, although less frequently.

A number of other characteristics of problem gambling need to be noted. Problem gamblers have a high incidence of insomnia, intestinal disorders, migraine headaches, and other stress-related disorders. Depression is quite common. About three-quarters of members of Gamblers Anonymous have been diagnosed as suffering from depression by a mental health professional at some time in their lives. Whether they gamble to relieve depression (as the *DSM-IV* criteria suggest) or whether depression is a result of their gambling (indebtedness, marital conflicts, job loss) is an unresolved issue.

Members of Gamblers Anonymous report an attempted suicide rate about six times as high as that of the general population. One study of 162 members of Gamblers Anonymous found that while 13 percent had attempted suicide, an additional 21 percent had seriously considered it.

Problem gamblers also exhibit some distinctive personality characteristics. While these are found among many problem gamblers, it must be remembered that not every problem gambler will exhibit all of them or exhibit them in an extreme way. There is considerable "diversity" among compulsive gamblers. Some are "action seekers" drawn to gambling for the excitement it offers. Others are "escape gamblers" who use gambling as an escape from a variety of personal problems.

Problem gamblers tend to be very intelligent, energetic, hardworking people who enjoy challenging tasks (handicapping races or sporting events, for example). They also tend to be narcissistic, arrogant, and very self-confident. After all, they believe that they can beat the laws of probability. They see themselves as "winners" and others as "losers" or "suckers."

Problem gamblers also have a need to control events. Gambling provides the illusion that they can control the uncontrollable. Some develop a kind of "irrational thinking," in which they come to believe that they can (literally) control the turn of a card, the roll of the dice, the spin of a wheel, or the outcome of a race. In the advanced stages of their disorder, especially when they see their financial problems as unsolvable and they become desperate, problem gamblers begin thinking backwards about their problems. Instead of seeing their financial, family, work, legal, and other problems as a result of their gambling, they see additional gambling as the solution to their problems.

What Are Problem Gamblers Addicted To?

Problem gamblers do not ingest, inject, or inhale substances as chemically addicted people do. Just what is it to which they become addicted? When we ask problem gamblers about this, the answer we get is "action." Action is an aroused, euphoric state involving excitement, tension, and anticipation of the outcome of a gambling event. It is the thrill of living "on the edge." Problem gamblers describe action as a "high" similar to that experienced from many drugs. Some experience these sensations when just thinking about gambling, as well as when they are actually gambling. Action also has been described as a "rush" that may include rapid heartbeat, sweaty palms, and even nausea. It is not uncommon for problem gamblers to describe being in action as "better than drugs and better than sex." When they are in action, they lose track of time and sleep; food, water, and using a bathroom become lower priorities than staying in action.

Cross Addiction. The view of problem gambling as an addiction is strengthened by a good deal of evidence that chemical dependency and problem gambling are related. About half of the members of Gamblers Anonymous and problem gamblers in treatment have had a serious chemical addiction (usually to alcohol) at some point in their lives and often for long periods of time. In addition, about 10 percent of people receiving inpatient treatment for alcohol and other drug addiction are problem gamblers.

Addiction "switching" also occurs. Counselors report that about 10 percent of recovering alcoholics replace their alcohol use with gambling, and about the same proportion of recovering problem gamblers become heavy consumers of alcohol.

How Prevalent Is Problem Gambling?

How big a problem is problem gambling? Since the mid-1980s, twenty-two general population surveys have been conducted in sixteen states, usually at the initiative of state lottery boards or gambling regulatory commissions. When we average the results of these surveys, it appears that about 4.3 percent of the adult population are problem gamblers (using the more inclusive meaning of problem gambling).

The work of the NGISC included having the National Opinion Research Center (NORC) at the University of Chicago conduct a national survey to provide an estimate of the prevalence of problem gambling. This survey included interviews with a random sample of 2,417 adults and 530 patrons of gambling facilities. The NORC study concluded that approximately 1.2 percent of the adult population (about 2.5 million people) met the *DSM-IV* criteria for "pathological gambling" and that an additional 1.5 percent (about 3 million people) were "problem gamblers."

Some evidence shows that the availability of gambling is related to the prevalence of problem gambling. "Replication" studies have been done in five states (New York, Iowa, Minnesota, South Dakota, and Texas). The results of these replications are somewhat mixed, but there is a pattern to them. The largest increase in the prevalence of problem gambling occurred in New York and Iowa. During the time covered, Iowa experienced a very substantial increase in the availability of legal gambling (mainly riverboat casinos), and New Yorkers had access to an Indian reservation casino in Connecticut, as well as casinos in Atlantic City. The problem gambling rate also increased in Minnesota where Indian reservation casinos opened. In Texas the increase was very small, and in South Dakota the prevalence of problem gambling actually decreased slightly. Overall, these replication studies support the conclusion that the more available and accessible gambling is, the higher the prevalence of problem gambling.

Why Is Problem Gambling a Hidden Addiction?

By now, the reader probably has formulated some answers to this question. Problem gambling is a hidden addiction for several reasons. Until very recently counselors who encountered problem gamblers for other problems have been unfamiliar with this disorder. Problem gambling has not been a topic covered in the professional education of counselors, and very few public or private human service agencies have had gambling treatment experts on staff. Hardly any members of Gamblers Anonymous report that they were referred to GA by a mental health professional. Those who have been treated by psychiatrists, psychologists, and counselors for other problems report that they were rarely asked about their gambling behavior.

Although problem gambling is similar to chemical dependency in many ways, it is much more difficult to detect because there are no physical signs of it as there are with addiction to alcohol or other drugs. You cannot smell problem gambling on a problem gambler's breath. A problem gambler's eyes do not dilate. Dice, chips, and cards do not leave marks on a problem gambler's arms. Problem gambling does not make you walk and talk funny, stagger, and fall down in a stupor the way excessive alcohol consumption can. Given all this, it is not surprising that problem gambling is a hidden, difficult-to-detect addiction.

The absence of physical signs of gambling addiction also makes it easy for the problem gambler to conceal and deny the problem. Those closest to the problem gambler—family, friends, and co-workers—can be easily deceived by him or her. Problem gamblers are skilled liars, and are very clever at concealing their gambling activities and gambling-related problems. The absence of physical signs of the addiction aids the problem gambler in maintaining the deception.

Finally, a low level of public awareness of problem gambling as an addiction and a disorder contributes to keeping it a hidden addiction. All too often, many people regard the problem gambler as just a "bad," "stupid," or irresponsible person. During at least the past fifty years, the medical profession, the mass media, and self-help groups have slowly developed awareness among the general public that alcoholism is a disease. Efforts to get problem gambling recognized as a real disorder are still in their infancy. We hope that it will not take as long as it did with alcoholism.

> "Heavy gambling is wrongly interpreted
> as an addiction. [It] is better understood
> as a leisure activity which is potentially
> dangerous."

Compulsive Gambling Is Not an Addiction

Michael Walker

Michael Walker is a professor of psychology at the University of Sydney and the author of *The Psychology of Gambling*. In the viewpoint that follows, he maintains that heavy or problem gambling is not an addiction. Whereas drug addicts become physically dependent on drug use, he argues, heavy gamblers do not become similarly dependent on the act of gambling. Walker believes that compulsive gambling is different from drug or alcohol addiction because gambling involves playing a game. Game players, he notes, often become obsessed with winning. Some people play slot machines habitually, he maintains, not because they are addicted to gambling but because they have convinced themselves that if they persevere they can eventually win a jackpot.

As you read, consider the following questions:

1. What is the author's opinion of the supposed withdrawal symptoms that follow the cessation of heavy gambling?
2. In Walker's view, why don't heavy slot machine players want to admit that they are playing the game in order to win money?
3. In Walker's opinion, what is ironic about labeling heavy gamblers as pathological?

Gambling is a common leisure activity in most countries and cultures throughout the world. However, it also attracts criticism and censure in most societies. Much of this criticism is directed at the fact that some gamblers continue with the activity to such an extent that it disrupts their lives, their families and their employment. Within western cultures, useful employment, family life and the acquisition of material wealth are central goals of the socialisation process. The heavy gambler is seen as a failure by these standards. One explanation for this failure is that the socialisation of the individual has been inadequate: the society has failed in its task. However, increasingly, a different kind of explanation is given: that the heavy gambler is ill. Heavy gambling is not only socially deviant but it is caused by a disease process in the individual. In particular, western societies are moving quickly to a recognition of heavy gambling as an addiction. At the same time there is a concerted attempt to change the concept of addiction itself. These two forces, one to classify heavy gambling as an addiction and the second to broaden 'addiction' to include heavy gambling, are converging on a view of heavy gambling as a pathological state of the individual.

In this viewpoint, it is argued that this view relies upon a strictly limited interpretation of the evidence. It is claimed that the view that heavy gambling is pathological is recent in origin and changing in character, that a pathology of gambling as an addiction has not been demonstrated, and that the similarities between drug addiction and heavy gambling are overstated. The movement to medicalise gambling as an addiction is not based on sound empirical evidence. Thus the inadequate metaphor of gambling as compulsive is replaced by another inadequate metaphor of gambling as addictive. What is required is a new, non-medical metaphor. . . .

The central question in understanding an individual predisposition to addiction concerns the actual mechanism that is different in the addicted person. In the case of alcohol consumption, there is evidence suggesting that the routes by which alcohol affects the neurotransmitters in the brain of the abuser are different from those for non-abusers. Whether or not these differences are confirmed and whether or not they can be extended to other addictive drugs, the possibility of such individual differences allows for a pathological or disease model for alcohol addiction. Clearly, a similar basis for a disease model of problem gambling cannot exist. . . .

Compulsive Gambling vs. Drug Addiction

In the case of drug addictions, the physiological effects of some drugs are known in some detail and the basis for physical dependence established. All addictive drugs act directly on the neurotransmission system and produce negative feedback loops whereby chemicals are manufactured by the body which act to minimise the disturbance induced by the drug. The withdrawal syndrome is simply the continuation of the action of these balancing chemicals when consumption of the drug ends.

In order to qualify as a behaviour which might be explained by similar processes, heavy gambling must first be demonstrated to have a withdrawal syndrome on cessation of involvement. The withdrawal symptoms following cessation of ingestion of opiates include trembling and shaking, heart-rate and blood-pressure changes, sweating and temperature changes, and difficulty in sleeping. Wray and Dickerson examined the recollections of compulsive gamblers belonging to Gamblers Anonymous in Britain, concerning how they felt in the first few weeks after stopping gambling. The majority gave answers suggesting relief and happiness at giving up. However, 30 per cent of the sample recalled some disturbance involving irritability, restlessness, depressed mood, poor concentration and obsessional thoughts. Symptoms such as these are mild and psychological compared to drug-withdrawal symptoms, which are frequently physiological and typically more severe. Such psychological symptoms might well be expected when a person gives up any exciting pastime that has consumed most of the waking hours over an extended period of time. Furthermore, even if irritability, restlessness, depressed mood, poor concentration and obsessive thoughts are present following the cessation of gambling, for these responses to qualify as withdrawal symptoms, it must be shown that they were not present prior to the onset of gambling. It is entirely possible that some gamblers are depressed prior to gambling and that the gambling itself relieves the symptoms which later return when the gambling is terminated. Such symptoms would be falsely assumed to be part of the withdrawal syndrome if appropriate control groups are not used. At this time, there appears to be no convincing demonstration of withdrawal effects following cessation of heavy gambling.

Although there may be other ways in which it is claimed that heavy gambling is similar to drug addiction, it is clear that claims of overall similarity are overstated. There is no adequate evidence that gambling involvement and drug addictions are similarly distributed in society, no convincing argument that people susceptible to problems with drugs are differentially susceptible to problems with gambling, and no pattern of withdrawal effects common to both. It is clear that gambling behaviour B has not been shown to be sufficiently similar to drug addiction A, for the claim that gambling is an addiction to follow as a matter of logic.

A New Perspective on Gambling

If we abandon the concept of gambling as addictive, how then shall we explain the fact that some gamblers do continue with the activity until they are financially ruined and every facet of their lives is detrimentally affected? And, if excessive gambling is not the same kind of thing as excessive consumption of psychoactive substances, what kind of thing is it? We need a genuine alternative to drug addiction as a schema that makes sense out of the paradox of persistence with an activity where the overt objective is winning money but persistence with the activity is a proven way of losing money. It is proposed here that the starting point for understanding gambling is not the insensate pleasure afforded by drugs but the sense of mastery that comes from striving at games of skill. The core idea is not 'addiction' but 'commitment'. The gambler is 'heroic', not 'hooked'. Perhaps he or she is also a fool, but then the same claim might be made about martyrs to causes everywhere. In expanding this metaphor, we could begin with any one of a number of more or less skilful activities. However, games of skill have a history as old as psychoactive substances, and have a number of attributes in common with gambling games. Among games of skill, the prototype is perhaps the game of chess.

Chess is a game of pure skill and therefore totally different from gambling games where chance predominates. Although the game is fully determined, the game tree is so large that there is no foreseeable time when even the most advanced computers will play perfect chess. The game therefore provides opportunities for humans to strive for mastery, where mastery is measured by success against opponents of increasing and measurable skill. Attempts to understand chess within a stimulus-response framework are doomed to failure, and the claim that people play chess for immediate pleasure, for excitement or for thrills are misguided. There are no studies of 'chess addicts' in the literature, yet chess can absorb a person's life as completely as heroin can consume the life of the drug addict. . . .

It is not claimed here that gambling games are games of skill but rather that gamblers approach the activity of gambling with the same kinds of motives, the same conviction that they will succeed, and proceed to develop their own special knowledge of the task as players do in games of skill. . . .

Gambling and Games of Skill

The fact that gambling occurs in the context of games of skill is the link between the heavy involvement in a game such as chess, which does not involve gambling, and games such as those offered by slot machines, which do not involve skill. Bridge, poker and blackjack are excellent examples of such games. There can be no question that they are games of skill: there are World Championships and World Champions, and the annals of each game contain legendary characters such as Georgio Belladonna, Amarillo Slim and Ken Uston. Each of the games supports professional gamblers as well as large numbers of devotees who aspire to becoming professional gamblers. And each of the games is able to absorb the life of a person, to become the focus of determined, persistent effort directed towards succeeding at the game.

Interestingly, there appear to be no studies of addiction to bridge, poker or blackjack and no therapies directed at relieving the 'compulsive' nature of the sickness. Nevertheless, there are people whose lives have been devastated by their involvement in these games. Attendance at meetings of Gamblers Anonymous will reveal that this is so. And regular attendance at any bridge club will bring contact with potentially productive professional people whose abilities have been wholly redirected to the game of bridge. Players of these games report characteristics such as loss of control and gambling larger amounts of money than intended that meet the criteria for pathological gambling.

Individuals Must Accept Responsibility for Their Behavior

It is time for at least some skepticism regarding the unquestioned need for addicts to admit powerlessness over their own behavior. It is worth considering whether such admissions constitute a self-fulfilling prophesy—that is to say, the belief that a habit is uncontrollable actually may discourage people from trying to stop behaving in a self-destructive manner since it is beyond their control. . . .

The debate about compulsive gambling, like that about other self-destructive or socially unacceptable behaviors ranging from compulsive drinking to compulsive shopping . . . , ultimately comes down to a single question: Should individuals who engage in these behaviors be excused on the grounds that they suffer from a disorder that produces urges they are unable to resist? Without further evidence, we believe the answer to be no.

Whether talking about newspaper employees who have a conflict of interest due to borrowing to pay off gambling debts, people who defraud banks and associates, or athletes who bet on games in violation of league rules, there should be no general moral or legal recognition or compulsive gambling disorder as a valid reason for such behavior.

Richard Vatz and Lee Weinberg, *USA Today*, November 1993.

Why are there not clinics for obsessional bridge, poker and blackjack gamblers? And why do these gamblers make up only a small fraction of the membership of Gamblers Anonymous? The answer probably lies in the fact that in these games there is a real element of skill. Persistence and immersion in the game can enable the gambler to play the game better. Since the game is played better, the risk of suffering the severe financial losses that characterise members of Gamblers Anonymous is reduced.

Gambling and Games of Chance

Numbers games are typically games without any opportunity of using strategy or developing skill. Although many numbers games are associated with problem gambling (lotteries, for example), one high-risk game from the perspective of problem gambling is the slot machine. If so-called 'compulsive' involvement in the play of slot machines can be explained in terms of persistence, determination, focused, goal-orientated activity then the whole range of gambling games and the whole range of gambling involvement can be explained without reference to addiction.

Slot machines are played for a wide variety of reasons, and it is more common than not for regular players to deny that they are trying to win money. Typically, players report playing the machines for amusement or excitement. Superficially, this result appears to favour an addiction model rather than a commitment model. However, a closer inspection of the play of slot machines leads to the conclusion that amusement or excitement as an explanation should be discounted. Since the likelihood of winning on the slot machine decreases with the length of time spent playing, regular players have essentially no chance of coming out ahead. Thus, for a regular player to admit to trying to win money would appear irrational to the player and to the observer. Attribution theory would lead us to expect that very few slot-machine players would view their motive for playing as an attempt to win money. Nevertheless, the operation of the machine is purely concerned with money in and money out. The reality of slot machines is that they are about the transfer of money. It is unreasonable to believe that any other aspect of the machine is of importance: one need only ponder how attractive to the regular player would be a slot machine that was played with monopoly money in and monopoly money out! Excitement is limited to the pay-out of large prizes and jackpots. For most of the time, playing the machine is not in itself an exciting activity.

It is likely that playing slot machines has other psychological functions for some players. Daley, for example, has argued that players are buying time on the machines. Such an idea has plausibility where playing the machine provides something of value to the player other than winning money. Older people are one group for which this account may be true. After retirement, and especially after the death of the spouse, the elderly have the problem of how to spend their time. For many elderly people, loneliness may be countered by the apparent sociability attached to playing slot machines in the company of others. It is not that playing the slot machine is a social activity but rather that the presence of so many others engaged in a similar activity provides a role and an explanation for their own lives. However, this is not the group that is most likely to suffer from involvement with slot machines.

Gamblers Build Up False Beliefs

If gambling is a goal-orientated activity like the acquisition of skill in chess, then the gambler is striving towards some goal. For the analogy to be useful, the goal must be identified and we must show that, in some sense, skill is being acquired. Since skilful play of slot machines would appear to be impossible, it is difficult to see how the goal-orientated nature of slot-machine playing could be a fact. The answer to this issue is at the heart of the claim that gambling does not conform to the characteristics of an addiction. The solution lies with the perceptions of the players. Slot-machine players believe they can influence the outcome of a machine. The evidence for this claim comes both from anecdote and from experiment.

Observation of slot-machine players shows that they do not behave as if all machines are equivalent. Players frequently can be seen searching out the machine that is close to a big pay-out or which is about to 'run hot'. A machine with certain pay-off structures, reels containing jokers, or multi-coin and multi-line machines may be chosen in preference to other varieties because of the opportunities for the use of skill. Some machines are preferred because the player can discern 'good vibes' or because it is 'known' to be close to a jackpot. And manufacturers recognise this belief in the ability to influence the machine by incorporating features which give the illusion that skill can be applied as in 'hold em' machines and accessories such as 'hole-in-one' bonuses. Seen from the perspective of the player, such beliefs are the basis of skill or special knowledge by which the machine can be influenced. Seen from the perspective of the observer, such beliefs are false. Whether or not the beliefs are true they can be elicited with ease and analysed statistically. What these studies show is that more irrational beliefs are expressed by players who play more frequently, and more so by slot-machine players than video-poker players. One straightforward interpretation of these results is that slot-machine players build up repertoires of false beliefs rather than real skills, and that these beliefs function in the same way, in relation to slot-machine games, as real knowledge or skill functions in relation to games where skill is possible.

Heavy Gamblers Are Perseverent, Not Addicted

From this perspective, the heavy slot-machine player is engaged in a contest with the machine. For some players, the contest attracts the same determination, perseverance and involvement that is afforded by other life-absorbing activities such as chess, bridge or computer games. They become immersed in the struggle, patient through failure, and convinced that ultimately they will succeed. The tragedy is that such commitment, that in other areas of life is applauded and to which many of us in western culture are socialised, is doomed to failure and bound to be financially hazardous. The loss of control which is often taken to be symptomatic of addiction is easily understood in terms of the beliefs of the gambler. The false beliefs held by the gambler persuade him or her that success is imminent. The financial outlay will be rewarded with persistence. The gambler is entrapped. To stop playing now is unthinkable when the jackpot is so much closer. Imagine how you would feel if the very next coin (not yours) won the jackpot. Thus it is not surprising that the play of the machine continues past all limits set by the gambler. Moreover, the slot machine provides small prizes quite frequently. These may well function to convince the player that the bigger prizes are near. Not surprisingly, heavy slot-machine players play a little faster following these rewards.

When asked after the event, the gambler will accurately report gambling more than intended and trying to cut down but failing. The combination of financial loss and lowered self-esteem associated with failure have effects on the gambler that have often been described.

Why does the slot-machine player not stop once it is clear that winning is not possible? There is perhaps a range of contributing factors. First of all, the slot-machine player may be convinced of the accuracy of his or her beliefs. Thus persistence will be rewarded. In any case the special knowledge required to defeat the machine is being acquired continuously in the course of testing new ideas. The mechanisms by which failure can be rationalised as success have been made explicit elsewhere. Beyond the special knowledge and skills that the player has gained there will be a network of friends and acquaintances that has been built up over time. They are engaged in similar endeavours and may function as a support to the legitimacy of the enterprise. Such networks have been described in detail for the racing game. Finally, when a person focuses their life on one activity or project, they become proficient in the activity in a way that may not happen in other parts of life. The slot-machine player knows all the roles, customs, norms and procedures in their environment. They know the history of machines, jackpots and players. It is in a broad sense their area of expertise. Although mastery of the game may be illusory, mastery of the environment is real. Such mastery contributes to the definition of self and is lost if the activity is given up. Nevertheless, where the financial losses are too great or the social pressure to desist from the activity too powerful, the slot-machine player may be forced to seek help. Although that help may come from agencies which accept the addiction perspective, the surprising fact is that alternatives exist for the gambler which would be unthinkable for the drug addict. . . .

The central claim in this viewpoint is that heavy gambling is wrongly interpreted as an addiction. Gambling is better understood as a leisure activity which is potentially dangerous. The danger is that persistence will cause heavy financial losses. The reasons why gamblers persist in the activity are not agreed upon. However, the dominant view among treatment agencies is that there is something wrong with the gambler who persists in the face of mounting financial losses. The view is that the gambler has become addicted to the activity. Addiction is understood as a pathology that afflicts certain people, and the heavy gambling that causes serious financial losses is defined as pathological. It is argued here that no pathology of the heavy gambler has been demonstrated that attempts to medicalise gambling as an addiction are based on the mistaken belief that drug abuse and heavy gambling are similar, and that gambling is better understood as a commitment of resources similar to that involved in success at games of skill. Attempts to install pleasure as the common ingredient of drug abuse and heavy gambling are misplaced.

It is ironic that the persistence displayed by the heavy gambler is lauded in other aspects of life. To work diligently, to play hard, to master hobbies, to acquire competence through practice, are part and parcel of successful socialisation in modern western industrialised societies. It is the heavy gambler who is labelled 'pathological' rather than the society in which diligence in one legitimate sphere is rewarded but in another punished. There are two main types of explanation for the plight of the heavy gambler who loses all assets: those which focus on individual weaknesses and those which take a broader social view. I have reviewed the explanation in terms of personal failure and concluded that there is no basis for attributing the phenomenon to pathology. Perhaps it is time to look again at the role of society and the preparation of the individual for modern life.

> *"The gambling industry has worked to make it easier to hook addicts and drain them of their money."*

The Gambling Industry Preys on Compulsive Gamblers

Bernard P. Horn

Bernard P. Horn is communications director of the National Coalition Against Legalized Gambling. The following viewpoint is adapted from his testimony before the National Gambling Impact Study Commission, a federal panel appointed in 1997 to study the social impact of legalized gambling. In it, Horn urged the commission to investigate the casino industry and state lotteries for evidence that they intentionally market their games to compulsive gamblers. Just as tobacco industry documents were made public in the early 1990s, proving that cigarette companies knew nicotine was addictive and intentionally marketed their product to minors, Horn believes that court-ordered subpoenas would force the gambling industry to turn over documents showing that they intentionally target compulsive gamblers.

As you read, consider the following questions:

1. What percent of gambling industry profits come from gambling addicts, according to the research cited by Horn?
2. In the author's view, what are some of the techniques that casinos use to drain gambling addicts of their money?

Excerpted from Bernard P. Horn's testimony before the National Gambling Impact Study Commission, August 20, 1997.

I am the communications director of the National Coalition Against Legalized Gambling (NCALG), a grassroots coalition of citizens and groups. Just like the sponsors and cosponsors of the legislation which created this Commission, we are Democrats and Republicans, liberals and conservatives, from every area of the United States. Let me emphasize that NCALG is not an organization of moralists. We are not trying to stop Americans from gambling. We do not seek to close down Las Vegas. But we are trying, through information and education, to stop the expansion of legalized gambling because the costs far exceed the benefits.

In my opinion the single most important action you can take is to use your subpoena power to uncover documents showing the extent to which gambling enterprises rely on addicts for their revenues.

As you know, litigants against the tobacco industry have used subpoena power to uncover documentation of what the industry knew about their product. They knew their product was addictive. They knew their profit margin depended on this addiction. And they seem to have responded by manipulating the addictive properties of their product.

Exploiting Addiction

We believe that documents exist which prove that the leaders of the gambling industry are also fully aware of the nature of their product. They know that many of their customers suffer from gambling addiction, a medically-recognized mental disorder. They know that a huge percentage of their profits are earned from gambling addicts. And they respond by designing gambling games and establishments in ways to encourage and exploit this addiction.

Some research in this area is already available. For example, Dr. Henry Lesieur compiled statistics from a number of studies which estimate the percentage of revenue that specific gambling games derive from pathological and problem gamblers. For the average gambling establishment in seven North American states and provinces, 30% of the profits come from the pockets of gambling addicts.

In fact, the gambling industry has worked to make it easier to hook addicts and drain them of their money. State lotteries, for example, have moved from once or twice-a-day sweepstakes to fast-paced casino-style keno and even slot machines. Slot machines now commonly include built-in bill acceptors so gamblers don't have to wait a few moments for change. Casinos now routinely include both ATM machines and cash-advance credit card machines right on the gambling floor.

The Gambling Industry's Political Clout

Gambling is a powerful political force.

Just how powerful? According to Timothy L. O'Brien, a *New York Times* reporter and author of the just-released Bad Bet, between 1991 and 1996, the industry put at least $4.5 million into national political campaigns. "That level of spending makes the gambling industry a political force at the federal level on a par with the National Rifle Association and the United Automobile Workers."

That's just the national level. Analysts guess as much as $30 million may have been spent dumping South Carolina Governor David Beasley. A Mother Jones study found that the industry gave more than $100 million in donations and lobbying fees to state legislators between 1992 and 1996. The industry's political muscle was on full display after the Clinton administration proposed in 1994 to fund new welfare programs by placing a 4-percent federal tax on gaming revenues. Thirty-one governors wrote in to condemn the idea. That number might be higher should such a stunt be attempted today.

American Prospect, March 1999.

How does the gambling industry know which tactics to pursue? By spending millions of dollars each year on research. Obviously the industry draws some conclusions from polls and focus groups. But there is psychological research as well. For example, the Colorado Lottery recently sponsored a study called "Mindsort," which analyzed the left and right sides of the human brain to understand how to manipulate player behavior. According to a March 1994 story in *U.S. News & World Report*, casinos use psychological research to learn how to keep their customers' senses stimulated with light, sound, action, and even color and smell. They speed up games, offer small payouts to keep customers trying, and design facilities to make patrons lose track of time—treating their customers as if they were rats in a cage.

This commission can do some helpful research with its appropriation, but far more valuable than that is the commission's sweeping power to subpoena virtually any document, item, or computer file in the country.

On behalf of the National Coalition Against Legalized Gambling, I urge you to use that subpoena power to obtain research already done but held in confidence by the gambling industry, especially the research that will prove the industry understands and actively exploits the mental disorder of gambling addiction.

"[The gambling industry] recognizes the importance of establishing and promoting responsible gaming practices."

The Gambling Industry Is Working to Reduce Compulsive Gambling

American Gaming Association

The American Gaming Association (AGA) is a trade group representing the casino industry. The following viewpoint is excerpted from the AGA's list of commonly asked questions about Responsible Gaming Education Week 2001, an event the AGA sponsors each year to promote responsible gambling and raise awareness of the problem of compulsive gambling. The AGA maintains that educating casino employees and the general public about the problem of compulsive gambling is one of the best ways to reduce the problem. The association also describes its support of the National Center for Responsible Gaming, which conducts scientific research on treatment for compulsive and underage gambling.

As you read, consider the following questions:

1. What are the two best ways for the casino industry to address compulsive gambling and underage gambling, in the AGA's view?
2. How much money has the casino industry committed to funding the National Center for Responsible Gaming, according to the AGA?

*Q*uestion: *What is Responsible Gaming Education Week?*
    Answer: Responsible Gaming Education Week was created by the American Gaming Association (AGA) to increase awareness of problem gambling among gaming industry employees and customers and promote responsible gaming nationwide. Held annually during the first week of August, Responsible Gaming Education Week is part of the AGA's Responsible Gaming National Education Campaign. Since its inception in 1998, the week has helped focus attention on this issue through companywide and industrywide contests; brochures, posters and other collateral material; seminars; and live satellite broadcasts and Webcasts.

Raising Awareness

Why does the gaming industry sponsor this type of event?
    The industry sponsors this event because it recognizes the importance of establishing and promoting responsible gaming practices and educating its employees and the general public about disordered gambling and underage gambling. According to scientific experts, the best way for the industry to help address these problems is through increased public education efforts and funding of additional peer-reviewed, independent research. This is one of the public education efforts undertaken by the AGA in response to those recommendations.

How serious is the issue of disordered gambling?
    Although the vast majority of people enjoy gaming as an entertainment option, there are those who do not gamble responsibly. While the number of people who don't gamble responsibly is relatively small, we believe that one problem gambler is one too many. We want to promote responsible use of our product through public education programs like Responsible Gaming Education Week.

What activities are the AGA and the gaming-entertainment industry undertaking during this week to educate the public about disordered and underage gambling and the importance of responsible gaming?
    This year's highlighted program is an educational video titled "Understanding the Odds: Risk and Probability in Gambling and Everyday Life." The video will address topics such as superstition and the "gambler's fallacy," while at-

tempting to put to rest some of the misperceptions that sur-
round not only gambling odds but also other types of events,
ranging from the probability of getting heads or tails when
flipping a coin to predicting the weather. It will be accom-
panied by activity sheets that can be used as part of an inter-
active group discussion following the showing of the video.
The video, based on an educational curriculum developed by
Harvard Medical School's Division on Addictions, will be
distributed to casino properties nationwide the week before
Responsible Gaming Education Week.

"People Are Going to Abuse It"

Interviewer: Answer those critics who say, these guys are
predators. . . .

J. Terrence Lanni, chairman of MGM Grand, Inc.: I think
the answer to that is one, I don't think of myself as a predator. As I've said, I don't know what the percentage is, but I
think even our opponents would say, that the vast majority of
people, who participate in the gambling, gaming, entertainment, resort experience are doing it in controlled states, well
within their means to enjoy themselves. And it's legal. And,
in my opinion, it's moral.

Now, for the people who abuse it, it's no different than if I
had a credit card company. There are people who are going
to abuse that. It's no different than if I owned one of the food
companies. People are going to abuse food. It's no different
than if I were working in—a Chief Executive officer of a major alcoholic beverage company. People are going to abuse it.

But do you deny the vast majority of the people, the enjoy-
ment of an endeavor? Because some people abuse it? I don't
think you do. I think what you do, is you forthrightly deal
with the people who have problems and you do your best to
help them.

Casino executive J. Terrence Lanni, interviewed on PBS's *Frontline*,
Spring 1997.

In addition, the AGA is making available on its Web site
a variety of promotional and informational materials to help
promote responsible gaming during the week. . . .

Why is there such an emphasis on educating employees?
The industry believes that employee education and involvement are critical to the success of Responsible Gaming

Education Week. Because so many of our employees inter-
act directly with customers, they need to learn about this issue and understand the importance of promoting responsible gaming practices. Employees will then transfer this
knowledge to the general public in the course of their daily
activities. Employee participation also will serve to involve
co-workers, family and friends, which will further raise
awareness of this issue. . . .

Sponsoring Research

*What else is the gaming-entertainment industry doing to combat
disordered gambling?*

In response to guidance from the scientific experts, the industry has emphasized two areas to help address disordered
gambling: public education and the funding of research.

Responsible Gaming Education Week is one of the many
public education activities undertaken by the AGA as part of
the Responsible Gaming National Education Campaign. The
industry also has published the *Responsible Gaming Resource
Guide*, a compilation of responsible gaming ideas, policies,
procedures and programs; conducted seminars and responsible gaming certification courses; developed a PROGRESS
Kit, which includes all the tools necessary for companies to
initiate a responsible gaming program; printed educational
and collateral materials to raise public and employee awareness of this issue; funded help-line phone numbers; and developed and distributed public service announcements.

In the area of research, the industry was instrumental in
founding the National Center for Responsible Gaming
(NCRG), the first nationwide funding source for scientific
research on disordered and youth gambling. Since its inception in 1996, the casino industry has committed $7
million in funding to the NCRG. The NCRG already has
awarded $3.2 million in grants, which are supporting
wide-ranging research in epidemiology, social and behavioral sciences, and neuroscience.

"The gambling addiction rate among teens is three times that among adults."

Compulsive Gambling Is a Serious Problem Among Teenagers

Tom Grey

Reverend Tom Grey is coordinator of the National Coalition Against Legalized Gambling. In the following viewpoint, he argues that young people are becoming addicted to gambling in record numbers. Like adult compulsive gamblers, Grey writes, teens hooked on gambling often turn to crime to support their habit, and some become suicidal when their debts become unbearable. He maintains that the spread of addictive forms of gambling such as video poker and the promotion of state lotteries and other forms of gambling by state governments have contributed to the problem. Moreover, Grey feels that young people are being drawn to gambling because adults have sent them a message that gambling is acceptable.

As you read, consider the following questions:

1. What percent of teens are pathological gamblers, according to the viewpoint?
2. What proportion of juveniles does Grey say has turned to crime to pay off a gambling-related debt?
3. What message does government promotion of gambling send to young people, in Grey's opinion?

From "The Diceman Cometh: Will Gambling Be a Bad Bet for Your Town?" by Tom Grey, *Policy Review*, March/April 1996. Copyright © 1996 by *Policy Review*. Reprinted with permission.

Flush with a handful of money he had just won at a bowling tournament, Joe Koslowski invited some friends to celebrate with him at the nearby Atlantic City casinos. Joe, then 16, and all his buddies were allowed in despite the age limit of 21. Once inside, Joe's good fortune continued; he parlayed his bowling winnings into a couple of thousand dollars.

After his initial success, Joe returned to the casinos frequently. His winning streak eventually ended, but his taste for the thrill of gambling did not. Once out of cash, he opened credit accounts under family members' names, using cash advances from the credit cards to gamble.

The whole scheme finally came crashing in on Joe last year, after he had amassed $20,000 in debt. Now at age 20, Joe, who had no prior criminal record, is serving time in a Pennsylvania federal prison for credit-card fraud.

Joe is one of tens of thousands of young people who fall victim to America's gambling obsession every year. At least three-quarters of the nation's teens engage in some form of gambling. Much of it, of course, is fairly innocuous and occurs among peers: weekend poker games, betting on football, the annual NCAA basketball tournament pool. Adolescents have become increasingly adept, however, at gaining access to state-sanctioned gambling—lotteries, casinos, electronic poker—which often becomes a bridge to compulsive or addictive behavior. In 1995, University of Minnesota researchers reported that more than half of underage Minnesota teens surveyed had participated in some form of legalized gambling. An earlier survey of Atlantic City high-school students revealed that nearly two-thirds had gambled at the city's casinos.

It is becoming painfully apparent that the only jackpot awaiting many of these young people is a life out of control.

More than a million adolescents are already addicted to gambling, according to Durand Jacobs, a clinical professor of psychiatry at Loma Linda University Medical School and an expert on youth gambling. Further, Jacobs says, the gambling addiction rate among teens is three times that among adults. In a recent review of major youth-gambling studies in North America, Howard Shaffer, director of the Center for Addiction Studies at Harvard Medical School, concluded that roughly one in six teens experiences gambling-related problems, while about 6 percent are actually addicted, or pathological, gamblers.

The New Jersey Council on Compulsive Gambling, which operates a national toll-free hotline, [reports that teen gamblers called] 4,300 times in 1994, accounting for 11 percent of total calls. Ed Looney, the council's executive director, says many of these young people find themselves in desperate straits. He tells of a call regarding a 16-year-old who had slit his wrists after losing $6,000—four years of newspaper delivery earnings—on the lottery in a single day. He tells of the college student from the Midwest who dropped out of school because he lost his tuition money gambling; of the 19-year-old New Jersey youth who sold his car for a fraction of its value so he could get back into the casinos; of the numerous calls from kids too scared to go back to school because they can't pay back their bookies.

The False Lure of Glamour and Wealth

The main reason teens get hooked on gambling is simply the lure of winning a large amount of money. According to Jane Haubrich-Casperson, author of *Coping with Teen Gambling*, teens "believe that instant wealth would change their lives for the better, help them acquire material things, and in many cases even help their families purchase life's basic necessities." In addition, she says, "Teenage gamblers want many of the things money can't buy: respect, adulation, praise, ego satisfaction. They [incorrectly] assume that these intangibles will come right along with the million-dollar prize.". . .

Television advertisements for state lotteries and gambling resorts such as those in Las Vegas also play a role in luring kids into gambling at an early age. Ads typically show glamorous people having fun and winning lots of money. Who wouldn't be attracted to such a picture? What the ads don't show are the many losers who go home with empty pockets.

Mark Rafenstein, *Current Health 2*, April 2000.

The phenomenon of youth gambling is not entirely new, but its rapid growth and startling magnitude is alarming. Says Valerie Lorenz, head of Baltimore's Center for Compulsive Gambling, "We never saw a teenage gambler 10 years ago. Now we see them regularly." Moreover, the most addictive forms of gambling—eagerly promoted by more and more state governments in search of tax revenue—can produce ripple effects in young lives that undermine families, communities, and civic order. As we move into the next century, Shaffer says, "We're going to have major issues with youth gambling that will equal or eclipse the problems that we have with substance abuse."

A Slippery Slope?

Experts draw a distinction between the "problem" gambler and the "pathological" gambler. According to Shaffer, pathological gamblers exhibit three basic characteristics: an inability to stop gambling despite massive losses, a sense of lost control, and a compulsion or craving to gamble. Problem gamblers can be affected in less severe ways, including difficulty concentrating, failure to fulfill family, school, or work obligations, general irritability, and sleeplessness. The two, however, are closely connected.

Shaffer refers to problem gamblers as being "in transition." [Gamblers] frequently move in and out of these designations. It is estimated that 1 to 3 percent of the adult population are pathological gamblers, but nearly twice that number are problem gamblers.

[Different forms of gambling have different attractions for] teens, as well as adults, though they vary in their potency. The most addictive, such as electronic poker, contain the element of rapid "action" and occur in relative isolation, Shaffer says. Video gambling and slot machines are inherently more dangerous than bingo or the lottery. But the lottery frequently serves as a gateway to other gambling activities for teens. Once exposed to even a relatively benign form of gambling such as the lottery, many find themselves craving greater excitement. Studies bear this out: Participation in other forms of gambling is higher in those states that have lotteries.

Many problem and pathological gamblers—adolescents or adults—become debtors. Once they get in over their heads, teen gamblers follow the cue of their elders: They turn to crime. Jacobs contends that at least one in 10 juveniles has used illegal means such as stealing, shoplifting, selling drugs, or prostitution to obtain money to pay off gambling-related debts. A 1994 study of Massachusetts youth found that 5 percent had been arrested for gambling-related problems.

Despite the extent and impact of youth gambling, Jacobs says, the level of public awareness is "absolutely abysmal." A few recent high-profile press reports, along with a meeting last spring of the North American Think Tank on Youth Gambling Issues at Harvard, have begun to bring the issue to the public's attention. Teens themselves remain largely unaware of the dangers associated with gambling. Shaffer found that only one-quarter of Massachusetts youth surveyed rated gambling as potentially dangerous, compared with 60 percent or more who perceived the dangers in alcohol, tobacco, and drugs.

Gambling in all its forms is proving to be nearly irresistible to a rising generation that frequently tells pollsters of its apprehensions about a bleak economic outlook. Traditional forms of gambling such as church bingo have generally been able to restrain compulsive betting. Government promotion of gambling, including the $350 million states spend advertising the lottery, has been more pernicious. It communicates to young people the subtly destructive notion that the work ethic is passe, that all they need is "a dollar and a dream." Perhaps that's why an average of 200,000 minors have been turned away from Atlantic City casinos every year for the past decade, according to figures from the New Jersey Casino Control Commission. Another 24,000 underage gamblers are escorted from the casino floor annually. Many more gamble in the casinos undetected. Ironically, many state lotteries are pitched to the electorate as a honey pot for public education.

"By sending young people the message that they need to gamble to get ahead," Shaffer says, "we're telling them not to study calculus, not to study science, and we shouldn't be surprised that America is now falling behind other cultures in terms of intellectual pursuits."

"State, private, charitable, and Indian gaming industry response to problem and pathological gambling needs to be more responsible."

The Social Costs of Compulsive Gambling Are Enormous

Henry R. Lesieur

Henry R. Lesieur is president of the Institute for Problem Gambling, author of *The Chase: Career of the Compulsive Gambler*, and an active researcher in the field of problem gambling. In the viewpoint below, he summarizes much of the research on the social costs of problem gambling. Financial loss and bankruptcy are some of the main costs of problem and compulsive gambling, notes Lesieur, and some gamblers turn to fraud or theft to pay their gambling debts. Compulsive gamblers also tend to have problems with their families and employers, and are more prone to various medical problems, psychological disorders, and addictions besides gambling. Lesieur concludes that efforts to prevent and treat compulsive gambling are not commensurate with the addiction's staggering costs to society.

As you read, consider the following questions:

1. According to the author, how much higher are attempted suicide rates among spouses of pathological gamblers, as compared to the general population?
2. Approximately what percentage of pathological gamblers does Lesieur say have also been diagnosed with major depressive disorder in their lifetime?

Excerpted from "Costs and Treatment of Pathological Gambling," by Henry R. Lesieur, *Annals of the American Academy of Political and Social Science*, v. 556, pp. 153(19). Copyright © 1998 by Sage Publications Inc. Reprinted with permission.

Embezzlement, family and job disruption, and other consequences of problem gambling have emerged as themes in society repeatedly over time. In the United States, while corruption played a dominant role in prohibition efforts, reformers in the nineteenth century rallied against the destructive impact of gambling on families, careers, and society in general. Their efforts eventually led to the suppression of gambling in the United States both in the 1830s and around the turn of the century. More recently, the National Coalition Against Legalized Gambling has pointed to problem gambling in an effort to stop the further spread of gambling legalization in the United States. Clearly, problem and pathological gambling have taken the front stage in the continuing debate over legalized gambling.

While reformers are having their day, national organizations (and their state or provincial affiliates) that act as advocates for problem gamblers and their families are having some impact as well. Affiliates of the National Council on Problem Gambling in the United States and the Canadian Foundation on Compulsive Gambling have been pushing for state-funded and provincially funded help lines, the education of treatment professionals, treatment for problem gamblers, awareness programs, and research into problem gambling.

Terminology and Epidemiology

The term "problem gambler" has been used in two ways: first, for those who have less serious gambling problems than pathological gamblers and, second, as an all-encompassing term to include both problem gamblers and pathological gamblers. This convention has its parallel in the alcohol and drug field in discussions of problem drinkers and substance abusers. Not all problem drinkers are alcoholics, and not all substance abusers are drug addicts. However, all alcoholics are problem drinkers, and all drug addicts are substance abusers. Consequently, with respect to the term "problem gambler," it is recognized that not all problem gamblers are pathological gamblers, but all pathological gamblers are problem gamblers.

Typically, the term "compulsive gambler" is used by the general public while the term "pathological gambler" is used by treatment professionals. This is because professionals reserve the term "compulsion" for behaviors like excessive hand washing and lock checking. Pathological gambling is classified as an "impulse control disorder" rather than a compulsion. . . .

As Legalized Gambling Becomes More Widespread, So Does Addiction

Experts on pathological gambling have shown that the prevalence of this disorder is linked closely to the accessibility and acceptability of gambling in society. Like alcoholism, just a small percentage of Americans are susceptible. As more people try gambling in its various forms, however, more of those prone to the illness are exposed. So, the more legalized gambling a state makes available, the more pathological behavior is triggered. Fast-paced gambling, which maximizes the number of wagering opportunities (like casinos and video gambling machines), also maximizes gambling addiction. In 1976, a national commission found that 0.77% of the adults in the U.S., about 1,100,000 Americans, were pathological gamblers. Today, the situation is far worse.

In Iowa, the legalization of casinos more than tripled the addiction dilemma. A study released in July, 1995, found that 5.4% of the state's adults (roughly 110,000 residents) are lifetime pathological or problem gamblers. Before river boats came to the state, 1.7% of Iowans fell into this category.

In Louisiana, four years after the state legalized casinos and slots, a study found that seven percent of adults had become addicted to gambling. In Minnesota, as 16 Indian casinos opened across the state, the number of Gamblers Anonymous groups shot up from one to 49.

Bernard P. Horn, *USA Today*, May 1997.

In 1974, 61 percent of the American population had gambled in the past year, and 71 percent had gambled in their lifetime; by 1988, these figures were 71 percent for the past year and 81 percent lifetime. More recent [1993] estimates from different states place the lifetime prevalence of gambling at between 74 percent in Georgia and 91 percent in Washington State. The combined rate of problem and pathological gambling in the 17 states where surveys have been conducted ranges between 1.7 and 7.3 percent. These studies show that the prevalence of problem and pathological gambling has increased in states where the availability of gambling has increased as well. They also show that problem and pathological gambling are more common among males, youths, and minority populations.

Financial Woes

From 18 to 28 percent of males and 8 percent of females in treatment and Gamblers Anonymous (GA) have declared bankruptcy. While most pathological gamblers do not declare bankruptcy, the amount of gambling-related debt (excluding auto loans, mortgages, and other so-called legitimate debt) found by some studies is staggering. For GA members surveyed [in 1996], this ranged from an average of $38,664 in Wisconsin (versus a median of $20,000) to an average of $113,640 in Illinois (versus a median of $18,000). Female GA members have a lower level of gambling-related debt, averaging $24,883. This is only the debt at entry into Gamblers Anonymous and does not include the debt they may have paid off previously. Lifetime gambling-related debts in Wisconsin averaged $61,000 ($25,000 median) and $215,406 ($45,000 median) in Illinois. Losses such as these inevitably place enormous stress on the gambler's family, work, and emotional life.

Marriage and Family Problems

The pathological gambler's financial burden is chiefly borne by the family. Added debt may mean that fewer family expenditures are possible. The mortgage, rent, gas, electricity, telephone, and other bills may be late or overdue. In extreme cases, utilities are shut off, automobiles or furniture is repossessed, household items are sold, and there is the possibility of being evicted from an apartment or experiencing a foreclosure on the mortgage. Added to this are patterns of lies and deception by the gambler; such patterns have been repeatedly documented in studies of gamblers and their families.

Spouses of pathological gamblers are harassed by bill collectors, experience insomnia related to gambling-produced difficulties, and have a wide range of stress-related physical problems, including chronic or severe headaches, intestinal disorders, asthma, and depression. They also have suicide attempt rates that are three times higher than those reported by the general population.

When compared with other groups of addicts (alcoholics and chemically dependent individuals), the marriages of pathological gamblers are not that different; however, the gamblers' families are less cohesive and less independent than those of control subjects. Other researchers have found that gamblers' families function more poorly than the general population with respect to problem solving, communication, family roles and responsibilities, affective involvement, and general functioning. It is no wonder, then, that 26 to 30 percent of GA members have gambling-related divorces or separations.

Problems at Work

At work, pathological gamblers experience a range of problems that depend on whether they are self-employed, employed in supervised jobs, or employed in unsupervised jobs. The lower the level of job supervision, the greater the chance that gamblers will exploit the time and finances the job possesses. They come in late after gambling, leave early to gamble, and use extended lunch hours and break time; they take sick days off for gambling and otherwise use available work time to gamble. Lateness and absences from work are produced by extended card games and casino ventures; lunch hours are lengthened to accommodate hours at off-track betting parlors. Between 69 and 76 percent of pathological gamblers state they have missed time from work due to gambling. Even while at work, the gambler's mind may not be on the job because of heavy losses, indebtedness, and intense efforts to get even; irritability and moodiness are added consequences.

Many gamble on company time; the activities include card playing, betting on numbers, and acting as a runner, writer, or bookmaker for a gambling operation at work. Fellow employees are borrowed from; advances are taken on paychecks; paychecks are garnisheed; and, as a last resort, the employee may steal from work or engage in illegal activities on company time. Gamblers who own businesses may exploit the business and drain its assets as well as those of suppliers and other creditors. Between 21 and 36 percent of gamblers in treatment or GA have lost a job due to their gambling.

Crime

Pathological gambling also results in illegal activities. Once pathological gamblers exhaust savings, rent money, credit cards, banks, credit unions, loan sharks, and other resources, they resort to quasi-illegal activities like loan fraud (borrowing under false pretenses), forging their spouse's signature on loans, and bouncing checks. Some become bookmakers or work in the illegal gambling world to finance their gambling. Further on they will embezzle from work, forge checks, engage in tax evasion and fraud, or otherwise engage in white-collar illegal activity.

The stress of gambling, the stress of financial pressures, the stress of family, and the stress of work combine to produce anxiety, depression, and cognitive distortions in the mind of the pathological gambler. The stresses impair judgement and decision-making processes and lead to crime. The [1995] Illinois survey found that the average amount stolen for 184 GA members was $60,700; the median amount stolen was $500, and 56 percent admitted stealing. The average in Wisconsin, excluding one person who took $8 million, was $5,738; 46 percent admitted stealing.

Medical Problems

Given the financial, marital, occupational, and legal problems, it is not surprising that in the later stages of their gambling, pathological gamblers experience depression, insomnia, intestinal disorders, anxiety attacks, cardiac problems, high blood pressure, migraines, and other stress-related problems. Two studies report on medical examinations of pathological gamblers. Russo, in a study of 217 successive admissions to the inpatient gambling treatment program at the Brecksville, Ohio, Veterans Administration Medical Center, uncovered 39 percent with major cardiovascular disorders; 26 percent with allergies; 17 percent with respiratory problems; 16 percent with nerve and sensory system disorders; 15 percent with musculoskeletal disorders; 43 percent with serious oral or dental disease; and 30 percent who were obese. In another systematic investigation, Bergh and Kuhlhorn uncovered fatigue, colds and flu, migraine headaches, gastric pain, nausea, and other physical problems in a study of 41 Swedish pathological gamblers.

Psychological Disorders

Pathological gambling overlaps with other disorders. Major depressive disorder is the one most commonly reported, with between 70 and 76 percent of pathological gamblers being given this diagnosis on a lifetime basis. High rates of hypomanic and bipolar disorder have also been found in some studies but not in others. There is some evidence that rates of depression are lower among pathological gamblers in the general population than in treatment samples but still higher than among controls and that it declines following treatment for pathological gambling. Panic and anxiety disorders have also been reported as occurring more commonly among pathological gamblers than in the general population.

In light of the high rates of anxiety and depression, it is no wonder that pathological gamblers have very high rates of suicidal ideation. Between 12 and 18 percent of GA members have made potentially lethal attempts at suicide; 45-49 percent have made plans to kill themselves; 48-70 percent have contemplated suicide; and 80 percent state they have "wanted to die."

Substance Abuse

Excessive substance use and chemical dependency are also common among pathological gamblers, with 47-52 percent of pathological gamblers receiving a substance abuse diagnosis. Conversely, between 9 and 14 percent of substance-abusing populations have been diagnosed as pathological gamblers. Studies of methadone populations have found similar results, with 9-20 percent diagnosed as pathological gamblers. Males were more likely to have gambling problems than females.

Antisocial personality disorder and narcissistic personality disorder have also been uncovered among pathological gamblers. . . .

The Need to Do More

In the past twenty years, gambling has increased, as has the rate of problem and pathological gambling. State revenues from gambling have increased exponentially, yet help for problem and pathological gamblers lags behind. Gross gaming revenues grew in the United States from $3.3 billion in 1974 to $44.4 billion in 1995, yet the total amount of money allocated by both the gaming industry and state governments to prevention, treatment, research, and public awareness for problem and pathological gambling was less than $20.0 million in 1997. Given that problem gamblers account for anywhere from 23 to 41 percent of gaming revenues, the minuscule amount allocated, less than 0.045 percent, is ridiculously low. One would think that the social costs are insignificant; however, as this viewpoint has documented, that is far from the case.

At present, legislatures and the gaming industry are paying lip service to the problem. What needs to be done? First of all, the National Gambling Impact Study Commission needs to seriously address the issue and not just submit a report that gets forgotten. That commission needs to call for a national institute on problem gambling, as there has been a National Institute on Drug Abuse and a National Institute on Alcoholism and Alcohol Abuse. Second, there is a need for a national clearinghouse on problem gambling. This could be administered by the national institute on problem gambling. Third, state legislatures need to fund prevention, awareness, treatment, and research.

State, private, charitable, and Indian gaming industry response to problem and pathological gambling needs to be more responsible. A responsible approach would involve (1) problem gambling awareness, prevention, and treatment programs for employees, their spouses, and their children; (2) continuing education and training of all personnel employed in the industry regarding problem and pathological gambling; (3) coordinated efforts among members of the industry to address the problem; (4) cooperation among industry leaders and councils on problem gambling to obtain state funding for prevention, awareness, treatment, and research; and (5) minimization of resistance to problem gambling research. Instead of challenging research findings, the industry needs to better fund researchers. A small start has been initiated through the National Center for Responsible Gaming. This is in its infancy, as funding—all from casino corporations to date—represents only 0.009 percent of gross casino revenues.

"*Opponents [of gambling] traffic in metaphors of invasion and addiction that define bettors as passive victims.*"

The Problem of Compulsive Gambling Is Exaggerated

Nick Gillespie

Nick Gillespie is editor-in-chief of *Reason*, a monthly magazine of politics and culture. In the following viewpoint, he maintains that the debate over legalized gambling has been biased by "horror stories" of compulsive gamblers whose lives have been ruined by their addiction. In reality, writes Gillespie, the vast majority of gamblers are normal people for whom gambling is not an obsession. The exaggerated view of compulsive gambling as a national epidemic, he argues, is promoted by antigambling zealots who want to ban legalized gambling because they feel it is immoral.

As you read, consider the following questions:
1. In Gillespie's view, what is the irony of the prohibitionist mind-set?
2. How has former leader of the Christian Coalition Ralph Reed described gambling, as quoted by the author?
3. According to the Harvard University study cited by the author, what percentage of Americans exposed to gambling can expect to become pathological gamblers?

It is common these days to chatter about smaller government and individual responsibility, but we are actually living in increasingly prohibitionary times. Choices properly decided by private individuals are instead being limited or abolished through restrictive public policy. Hence, the V-Chip, government-mandated ratings of television programs, and attempts to regulate information flow on the Internet; federal- and state-level attempts to regulate cigarettes as "nicotine-delivery devices"; and a reinvigorated War on Drugs. . . .

The latest target of prohibitionists is legalized gambling, which has enjoyed a decade or so of rapid growth. [In the mid-1980s], only Nevada and New Jersey boasted casinos. Nowadays, there are two dozen states with casinos, including betting houses run by 126 different American Indian tribes. Thirty-seven states run lotteries and some have either allowed or are considering slot machines at existing gambling sites such as horse- and dog-racing tracks. [In 1995], Americans spent more than $40 billion on legalized gambling, up from about $10 billion in 1982.

The anti-gambling backlash is here, there, and everywhere. [Since 1994], the National Coalition Against Legalized Gambling (NCALG) has stymied casino and slot-machine plans in 23 states. The backlash is worth pausing over not only because it threatens yet another personal liberty but because it also allows insight into the prohibitionist mindset.

Prohibitionists are in the difficult position of telling people that certain choices are so misguided that they simply can no longer be allowed. But since the targeted behavior is usually highly popular and widespread, prohibitionists must redefine it as an unconditional evil that cannot be resisted, even by men and women of character. Ironically, in the name of morality, prohibitionists must strip individuals of the right to make moral decisions.

This is certainly the case with gambling, where opponents traffic in metaphors of invasion and addiction that define bettors as passive victims. The Reverend Tom Grey, the Methodist minister who heads the NCALG, describes himself as "a man committed to all-out war" against the "predator" gambling industry. The middle Americans who fill the casinos, you see, don't really want to spin the wheel, throw the dice, or take the chance. [Conservative politician] Pat Buchanan rails that "gambling should return to the swamp whence it came," ignoring the fact that 125 million Americans willingly choose to go to casinos every year.

Reasons for Gambling

Question: Please tell us . . . whether each of the following reasons was very important, important, not so important, or not at all important to you as a reason for gambling . . . the excitement or challenge of gambling . . . to socialize with family and friends . . . to win money.

(This table summarizes the responses of those who chose "important" or "very important.")

	Excitement/ Challenge	To socialize	To win money
Total	40%	36%	65%
Sex			
Male	43	36	66
Female	36	35	64
Race/Ethnicity			
White	41	36	63
Black	37	29	78
Hispanic	34	43	65
Age			
18 to 29	51	43	72
30 to 39	42	34	66
40 to 49	35	39	65
50 to 64	32	32	60
65 and older	33	33	56
Education			
Less than high school	32	36	63
High School Graduate	41	33	71
Some College	39	33	65
College graduate	41	41	60
Income			
Less than $24,000	35	36	64
$24,000 to $49,9999	43	34	69
$50,000 to $99,999	42	37	62
More than $100,000	40	39	65

Survey by NORC for the National Gambling Impact Study Commission, September 8–December 15, 1998.

The Christian Coalition's [former executive director] Ralph Reed pronounces gambling a "cancer on the body politic, destroying families, stealing food from the mouths of children, turning wives into widows." Betting as rapacious disease? That would have been news to the folks I used to ride with on infrequent trips to Atlantic City during the '80s. We gambled because it's fun to do, every once in a while. Forty or 50 people—college kids, vacationers, retirees—would pile in a bus in midtown Manhattan and ride a couple of hours to play slots and cheap blackjack. When it came time to leave, no one, to my knowledge, ever had to be pried away from the roulette table or the slot machines.

The Problem of Compulsive Gambling Does Not Justify Prohibition

A multitude of devils plague modern life. Gambling is one, perhaps, to some people but not to the majority and is by no means the source of all evil. In the context of a basically healthy society the question of whether to allow commercial gambling should not, as many clinical researchers and social critics argue, be decided solely in terms of the potential risk of increased compulsive gambling. Compulsive gambling is only one of the factors that should weigh in the decision to legalize. Without in any way minimizing the problem of compulsive gambling for affected individuals, it does not seem to us to constitute an unacceptable social risk of legalizing activities most Americans clearly approve of and enjoy without incurring unaffordable losses.

Vicki Abt, James F. Smith, and Eugene Martin Christiansen, "Misconceptions Abound in the Debate over Legalized Gambling," in Rod L. Evans and Mark Hence, eds., *Legalized Gambling: For and Against*. Chicago: Open Court, 1998.

Indeed, the social scientific literature, including studies done for the Swedish, British, and U.S. governments, tends to characterize gamblers as virtually indistinguishable from non-gamblers—except that gamblers are more sociable, more involved in community activities, and bigger opera, theater, and museum buffs. While it is true relatively poorer people spend more proportionally on wagers and bets, the overwhelming majority of gamblers responsibly budget their expenditures and use their winnings for "home-centered items."

The profile of gamblers as normal people, however, is unlikely to work its way into many stories about anti-gambling activism. Rather, the media showcase the dark side of gambling. A recent *Time* story, for instance, recounts the fate of a 40-year-old school teacher and mother of two who shot herself in the head after racking up huge gambling debts. "The day she died," writes *Time*, "sheriff's deputies were on their way to her home with an eviction order. . . . [H]er husband . . . knew nothing of their financial problems, although she had pawned their wedding rings and skipped making the house payments for 17 months."

Such a story is, of course, undeniably tragic—and undeniably rare. *Time* itself mentions in passing that Harvard University's Center for Addiction Studies estimates that "between 3.5 percent and 5 percent of all adults exposed to gaming can be expected to develop into pathological gamblers." Other estimates are lower still.

Horror stories, however bleak, should not guide public policy. "Gambling," note Reuven and Gabrielle A. Brenner in their 1990 history *Gambling and Speculation*, "is a mass phenomenon, and its study must not be confused with that of a pathological minority of compulsive gamblers, just as the examination of a few workaholics, alcoholics, obese people, womanizers, addicted TV watchers, and addicted exercisers is irrelevant for a social judgment on the behavior of the billions who work, drink, eat, love and/or have sex, watch TV or enjoy exercising with customary frequency."

For prohibitionists, of course, the self-regulation evinced by better than 95 percent of gamblers is a logical impossibility or, perhaps, a logical improbability. The world confounds prohibitionists, as do people who believe they should decide how to live their own lives.

Periodical Bibliography

The following articles have been selected to supplement the diverse views presented in this chapter. Addresses are provided for periodicals not indexed in the *Readers' Guide to Periodical Literature*, the *Alternative Press Index*, the *Social Sciences Index*, or the *Index to Legal Periodicals and Books*.

Richard Amberg — "Addicted to Lotteries," *Insight on the News*, September 20, 1999.

Jane E. Brody — "Compulsive Gambling: Overlooked Addiction," *New York Times*, May 4, 1999.

Christian Science Monitor — "States and Problem Gamblers," February 29, 2000.

Kevin Clarke — "We're Gambling with the Future," *U.S. Catholic*, July 1999.

Dale Eisler — "Hooked on the Game," *Maclean's*, January 9, 1995.

Samuel C. Gwynne — "How Casinos Hook You," *Time*, November 17, 1997.

Bernard P. Horn — "Is There a Cure for America's Gambling Addiction?" *USA Today*, May 1997.

Timothy C. Morgan — "The Invisible Addiction," *Christianity Today*, April 8, 1996.

Marc N. Potenza et al. — "Pathological Gambling," *Journal of the American Medical Association*, July 11, 2001.

Brett Pulley — "Those Seductive Snake Eyes: Tales of Growing Up Gambling," *New York Times*, June 16, 1998.

Ronald A. Reno — "The Diceman Cometh," *Policy Review*, March/April 1996.

Joshua Wolf Shenk — "Is Legalized Gambling Becoming Unsinkable?" *U.S. News & World Report*, August 4, 1997.

USA Today — "Compulsive Gambling May Be Inherited," April 1999.

Richard E. Vatz and Lee S. Weinberg — "Refuting the Myths of Compulsive Gambling," *USA Today*, November 1993.

CHAPTER 3

How Does Legalized Gambling Affect Communities?

Chapter Preface

In the 1990s, several states attempted to rejuvenate local economies through gambling. Previously sleepy towns such as Deadwood, South Dakota, and Gary, Indiana, suddenly became home to glitzy Las Vegas–style casinos. In each of these towns there was considerable debate over how legalized gambling would affect the community. These debates continue years after the casinos have opened.

In 1991, voters in Tunica County, Mississippi—then one of the poorest counties in the United States—approved casino gambling in the hopes of generating some much-needed revenue. Tunica's first casino opened in 1992, and ten others soon followed.

The economic effect gambling has had on Tunica has been astonishing. The casinos have generated more than fourteen thousand jobs. Taxes on the casinos bring the county more than $36 million a year. So far that money has been used to build two new schools, miles of new roads, a river park and marina, an airport, and much more. In 1999 Tunica even abolished its property tax because the casinos generate more than enough to meet the county's needs. "The gambling industry has been the only thing that has had a positive impact on Tunica County over the last 50 years," says John E. Gnushke, an economist at the University of Mississippi.

Despite this wealth, Tunica's population is still only about ten thousand. Most of the fourteen thousand new casino jobs have been filled by people living in neighboring counties. Tunica still has no major grocery store, drug store, or movie theater, and its public schools still have the lowest test scores in the state. "Tunica still produces little except cotton and catfish," writes the *Tampa Tribune*, "since gambling produces so few winners, it seems to be perpetuating the trend that's been going in the area since the days of slavery: a few people getting rich off of the misery of others."

Tunica is just one example of a community in which legalized gambling has had either astounding or disappointing results, depending on one's point of view. In the following chapter, authors debate whether legalized gambling benefits or harms communities.

"With few exceptions, legalising gambling has failed to stimulate the expected economic miracle."

Legalized Gambling Harms Local Economies

Economist

The *Economist* is a weekly international news and business publication that offers reporting and commentary on a wide variety of issues. In the following viewpoint, the editors of the *Economist* argue that legalized gambling is not an effective tool for economic development. Throughout the 1990s, the viewpoint explains, states across America legalized casino gambling in the hope that it would benefit the local economy by increasing tourism. But according to the *Economist*, most of these new casinos are patronized by locals, who spend their money on gambling rather than on buying goods from other businesses. There is thus no net benefit to the local economy. Furthermore, according to the viewpoint, communities that legalize gambling incur substantial social costs—in the form of problem gambling and crime—which are ultimately paid for by taxpayers.

As you read, consider the following questions:

1. What are some of the "negative externalities" associated with legalized gambling, according to the authors?
2. In the *Economist*'s view, why is Las Vegas a misleading model for other cities considering legalized gambling?

In 1995, 177 million Americans went to watch the baseball, football, hockey and basketball matches, not to mention golf tournaments and car races, that make up what most people think of as away-from-home entertainment. Yet almost as many Americans, 154 million of them, walked through the doors of the country's casinos. Americans in 1995 wagered an eye-popping $550 billion on all forms of gambling, handing the gambling industry a record $44.4 billion in profits, 11% more than the previous year. Around 40% of that activity took place in casinos. On the face of it, casino gambling has become the most popular leisure activity—well, maybe the second most popular—in America.

It is at least as popular with Wall Street and American business. [Since 1995], Goldman Sachs and Morgan Stanley, two blue-chip investment banks, have set up research and banking teams to serve the "gaming and leisure" industries, as the gambling organisations like to be called. Respectable firms such as Hilton Hotels and ITT have acquired casino operators. Las Vegas and Atlantic City are expanding faster than ever before. To all appearances, casino gambling is a rich, successful and untroubled business.

It may seem strange, then, to argue that America's love affair with casinos is essentially over. Strange, too, to assert that the gambling industry is largely responsible for ensuring its own eventual decline. But there is growing evidence for both arguments. And the irony is that the roots of gambling's failure lie not only where one might expect—in moral objections—but in the consequences, expected and unexpected, of the economic success which helped the casinos' emergence into respectability. . . .

The False Example

To understand the reason for casino gambling's coming failure, start with the reason for its success. In the 1940s, when Bugsy Siegel turned to Las Vegas as the place to set up a gambling empire, he made a shrewd guess: if you build a casino in the desert, people will flock to it. After a shaky start, the experiment proved a success. That was in part because Las Vegas at the time had a country-wide casino monopoly (the next casinos, in Atlantic City, New Jersey, were not approved until 1976).

The frenzied expansion of Las Vegas in the late 1980s and early 1990s caught the politicians' eyes. So too did the economic impact of casinos on equally isolated Indian reservations. As sovereign nations, tribes were for a long time allowed to run gambling operations when these were forbidden elsewhere. In the early 1990s, the economy of many parts of the country was stagnating, and state politicians were under pressure either to cut services or to raise taxes. Many suddenly had the same idea. Why not legalise casinos, thereby creating employment as well as a firm base for future taxes on the profits of the chosen local monopolist?

Gambling firms were quick to share the idea, promising lavish improvements in the infrastructure of run-down urban centres. Would-be operators of new casinos talked smoothly of repaved streets, splendid shops and thriving "eateries". And the politicians, for their part, found a further way to draw attention to the supposed advantages of legalised gambling. They could earmark gambling-tax revenues for some of the things voters wanted: for example, by 1991 13 states, including New York and California, had allocated some or all of their lottery receipts to education.

Look at Connecticut. Few states have had more bruising battles over whether to extend casino gambling. But since 1992 Connecticut has been home to America's most successful casino, Foxwoods, which sits on land belonging to the Mashantucket Pequot tribe of Indians. Thanks in part to the fact that 22 million people live within 150 miles of Foxwoods, the casino gets around 45,000 visitors a day and makes an estimated daily profit of $1 million.

Not surprisingly, other gambling interests have sought a share of the Connecticut pie. In the early 1990s, Steve Wynn, chief executive of the Mirage Corporation, a big casino operator, tried to win casino licences in Connecticut's state capital, Hartford—which has suffered from the decline of the big insurance firms that once dominated its economy—as well as in the decrepit town of Bridgeport. Despite generous spending, and his gleaming vision of what gambling would do for the economy, both of Mr Wynn's attempts failed. Yet casino operators are still seeking other places to expand. A lively debate is going on at present over proposals to legalise casinos in New York, specifically to draw "the gambling dollar" away from New Jersey and Connecticut.

How the Reality Dawned

The trouble, as some New York legislators are pointing out, is that the supposed casino miracle has two big problems in practice. First, with few exceptions, legalising gambling has failed to stimulate the expected economic miracle. According to Harrah's Casinos, which publishes an annual survey of the industry, casinos employed 367,000 people in 1995, more than half of them in Nevada. That was a 24% increase since the start of 1994. But the jobs created by the arrival of casinos are too often menial—money-counters, cleaners—and have all too often been cancelled out by the jobs that are lost as the newcomers drive older firms out of business. Moreover, bare statistics that show the growth of gambling jobs ignore the job creation that would have happened in the absence of a casino.

The Cannibalization Effect

Staking the future on gambling, economists argue, could only work in a fantasyland. It's an industry that produces no product and no new wealth, and thus makes no genuine contribution to economic development. "Governmental officials are increasingly being enticed to accept and then impose upon the public those discredited economic philosophies which claim that gambling activities increase jobs, foster economic development, and generate new tax revenues—all without raising taxes on the electorate," says University of Illinois economist John Warren Kindt. "In reality, the regional and strategic impacts of legalized gambling almost invariably result in a net loss of jobs, increased taxes, and negative economic spiral which is inherently recessionary. . . . Furthermore, the net creation of jobs claimed by the legalized gambling industry is at best a break-even proposition, and the evidence suggests that net job losses can easily occur—primarily because 'consumer dollars' are drained from the rest of the economy. The literature frequently refers to this process as 'cannibalization.'"

Jennifer Vogel, ed., *Crapped Out: How Gambling Ruins the Economy and Destroys Lives.* Monroe, ME: Common Courage Press, 1997.

Belatedly, the politicians who welcomed casino gambling for its economic spin-offs have realised that it takes more than a few superficial improvements to revitalise a struggling city centre. Moreover, as more and more casinos have opened, so competition has diminished the amount of business each one can expect. The once-sunny economic projections have faded. In Deadwood, South Dakota, for example, an initial flush of profitability was destroyed by the speedy arrival of dozens of competing casinos, so that bust quickly followed boom.

Second, many places failed to understand that casinos, more than other forms of gambling such as lotteries, cause what economists call "negative externalities". There is a price to pay in the rising cost of such things as law enforcement, street cleaning and (some argue) the extra social services needed when gambling leads to the break-up of families. When these additional costs are taken into account, it is far from clear that gambling benefits anyone except the casino operators.

Las Vegas Is Unique

Both these problems were predictable. It was naive to extrapolate from the success of Las Vegas a guaranteed economic stimulus for any city that opened its doors to a casino. Robert Goodman, a professor at Hampshire College in Massachusetts who writes on the economics of the gambling industry, argues compellingly that Las Vegas was a misleading model for the rest of America. To experience the seedy glamour of that city in the desert, most visitors have to come from a long distance away. A trip to gamble therefore becomes a full-scale holiday, complete with a stay in a hotel, visits to local restaurants and no doubt a little shopping thrown in. In Las Vegas, casinos genuinely support the service economy.

Contrast this with, say, Atlantic City in New Jersey. The place is a bus ride away from New York City, and perhaps 30 million people live close enough to visit its casinos for a day at a time. Many even cut their own sandwiches at home; they are the "brown-bag gamblers". As is all too evident in the seedy downtown area with its paucity of restaurants, Atlantic

City collects relatively few non-gambling dollars.

The contrast is greater still in places such as Joliet, Illinois, or Gary, Indiana. There is little in such cities to attract visitors from any distance away. It is the locals upon whom the casinos have to rely. Earl Grinols, an economics professor at the University of Illinois, points out what this means. Because local people are spending money on gambling that they would otherwise have spent on, say, buying clothes or going out for a meal, many non-casino firms suffer from reduced turnover and profits. This not only limits the number of people they employ; it also means that they pay proportionately less tax to local and state governments.

Similarly, many of the people employed by a casino live outside the city where the casino is sited—and spend their money outside it, too. Nearly 60% of the staff of Joliet's casino live outside the city, and half of those outside the county. This does not mean that nobody benefits. In Joliet, nine people paid some $7 million for the town's casino franchise. Their investment paid for itself in six months, and each now collects a monthly dividend of some $900,000.

At last, it has started to dawn on the rest of the city's people that the economic benefit from a casino depends largely on where it is. Add the fact that, the more casinos there are, the smaller the share of America's gamblers any one of them will be able to attract, and it is plain how the dreams have been punctured. Even the gambling industry, which used to boast of the market's almost infinite potential, has become more circumspect. Casino firms have begun to consolidate as stronger competitors buy weaker ones. And industry analysts say that these days the growth prospects of many "gaming" firms come more from non-gambling sidelines (such as food, shops and shows featuring well-known crooners) than from gambling itself.

The Price of Gambling

As casinos have failed in many cases to revive local economies, so something else has happened. The old moral doubts about gambling, which were swept under the carpet when it seemed to offer a key to success, have resurfaced. In the process, whatever respectability gambling had recently acquired has been eroded.

Gambling-related social costs are extremely difficult to quantify. Nevada has the highest suicide rate in America; it also has among the highest number of accidents per mile driven, and deplorable crime and high-school drop-out rates. New Mexico, however, which is almost free of casinos, can rank alongside Nevada on all these counts. A causal link between gambling and these indicators is hard to prove. But it is becoming easier to establish that damage is done by gambling in general and by casinos in particular, largely because they contain slot machines, which are highly addictive.

Perhaps one-third of adult Americans never gamble, reckons Mr. Grinols. Many people who do are cautious. But a small percentage, perhaps 2% or 4% of America's adult population, are "problem" or "pathological" gamblers, and these account for a disproportionately large share of the activity's costs. One study in Minnesota found that 10% of bettors accounted for 80% of all money wagered.

Their numbers may be small; but their impact is not. Problem gamblers have a high propensity to commit crimes, in particular forgery, theft, embezzlement and fraud. These crimes affect both immediate family and colleagues at work. The American Insurance Institute estimates that 40% of white-collar crime has its roots in gambling. Gamblers often descend in a spiral of increasingly desperate measures to finance their habit in the hope of recouping their losses. Further, even before they turn to crime, problem gamblers are unproductive employees, frequently absent or late and usually distracted. A 1990 study in Maryland estimated that the state's 50,000 problem gamblers accounted for $1.5 billion in lost productivity, unpaid state taxes, money embezzled and other losses.

All taxpayers contribute towards the cost of policing, judging and incarcerating criminals. Casino gambling increases those costs. Since the Foxwoods casino opened in 1992, one police chief in a small Massachusetts town two hours' drive away reckons that local crime related to the casino has cost some $400,000. Multiply that figure by thousands, and the national impact of casino gambling begins to emerge.

The Casino Industry's Response to Problem Gambling

Are casinos alone to blame? After all, gambling in America extends far beyond crap tables and slot machines. State governments themselves encourage gambling by spending millions to advertise lottery jackpots on television. But not all forms of gambling are equal: in Minnesota, for instance, two-thirds of people seeking help for their gambling problems blamed casinos for their addiction. A mere 5% cited lotteries.

The casino industry itself acknowledges its role in the problem. The American Gambling Association helps to finance a national Centre for Problem Gambling. Several firms promote programmes designed to help gamblers kick their addiction, and most casinos post free telephone numbers where people can find help. Gambling interests have also suggested that tax revenues from casinos could be used to pay for treatment for recovering gamblers. But even on conservative measures (reached by assuming that the average casino visitor loses $200 annually), problem gamblers would account for three-eighths of casinos' revenues. How badly does the industry want to cure them?

All this is potent evidence that casinos are a bad bet. But even if the effects of problem gambling are discounted, the fact remains that casinos are not a development tool, either. The risk—which everyone was aware of at the outset—is not paying off. Without resorting to moralising, and even without mentioning organised crime, those who would clamp down on gambling can now make a formidable economic case.

"Casino gaming creates jobs and reduces the level of unemployment and government assistance in communities that have legalized it."

Legalized Gambling Benefits Local Economies

Frank J. Fahrenkopf Jr.

Frank J. Fahrenkopf Jr. is president and chief executive officer of the American Gaming Association (AGA), a trade group representing the casino industry. In the following viewpoint, Fahrenkopf disputes claims that legalized gambling harms communities. On the contrary, he argues that the casino industry benefits local economies by creating jobs and paying taxes to local governments. Fahrenkopf also disputes the idea that the spread of legalized gambling has caused an increase in compulsive gambling, and he describes the AGA's efforts to prevent and treat compulsive gambling. Finally, Fahrenkopf maintains that gambling does not cause increases in bankruptcy or crime in communities where casinos are legal.

As you read, consider the following questions:

1. What were some of the National Research Council's findings from its study of the economic effects of legalized gambling, as quoted by the author?
2. What national foundation has the AGA opened in response to concerns about pathological gambling?
3. What conclusion did the U.S. Treasury Department reach regarding the relationship between bankruptcy and casino gambling, as quoted by Fahrenkopf?

Excerpted from "The Gaming Industry: Current Legal, Regulatory, and Social Issues," a speech before the ALI-ABA by Frank J. Fahrenkopf Jr., www.americangaming.org, March 29, 2001. Copyright © 2001 by The American Gaming Association. Reprinted with permission.

My organization, the American Gaming Association, is the trade organization representing the commercial casino industry. While commercial casino gaming is legal in 11 states—Nevada, New Jersey, Mississippi, Louisiana, Indiana, Missouri, Illinois, Iowa, Colorado, Michigan, and South Dakota—the AGA's role is national in scope. We represent casino operators, along with equipment manufacturers, suppliers and vendors, financial services companies, and others that work with the gaming industry, on federal legislative and regulatory issues that affect our business.

But we have another important mission: to serve as an information clearinghouse—a truth squad of sorts—to correct the many misperceptions about our industry. We're all familiar with the colorful history of this business. Some people still believe this is the way we operate. But it is precisely because of this past that the gaming industry now operates in a legal and regulatory environment unlike any other industry. Every aspect of our business—from the hours we operate to the people we employ—is monitored and enforced.

Despite these safeguards, which make our industry one of the most scrutinized in the country, those opposed to gaming like to perpetuate misinformation in an effort to turn back the clock. I would like to share a little about this environment—the environment that will face anyone involved in the business of gaming.

Let me start by giving you a snapshot of the social issues that have swirled around this industry for years, as well as an overview of the latest research on this topic. Fortunately, a lot of good, *independent* research has been done recently that disprove nearly everything opponents of our industry have ever said about our business. The most comprehensive study in the past 20 years on the subject of legalized gambling was completed in 1999 after a two-year federal commission appointed by Congress conducted a comprehensive, legal and factual study of the social and economic impacts of gambling on federal, state, local, and Native American tribal governments, and on communities and social institutions. The final report of the National Gambling Impact Study Commission (NGISC) addresses many of the issues the industry faces, and I would urge you to get a copy and familiarize yourself with it. It's important for you to be aware of all this information so you can counter their attacks with *facts*.

For years, anti-gaming advocates had been selling the American people, media and decision makers a defective bill of goods based on so-called economic theories with no basis in fact. That bill of goods faced intense public scrutiny for the first time ever during the commission's deliberations. Today, I'd like to give you an overview of what the commission heard to refute that and add what the latest independent research reveals.

Let's start with the morality argument. The United States is a wonderful country where a divergence of opinion is not only tolerated but encouraged. The United States and Canada share a common ancestral heritage with England. But as you are probably aware, the first settlers in our country were the Puritans—religious extremists of their era. In some ways, this cultural heritage still manifests itself today. And so there are many who find what we do immoral. So be it. Nothing we can say or do will change their minds. While we respect their right to maintain their moral views, the fact is *they are not shared by the vast majority of Americans.* The latest polling data says that more than 80 percent of Americans believe that casino gambling is acceptable for themselves or others. And U.S. households visited casinos more than 162 million times last year.

Even the most religious Americans believe in the public's right to choose whether or not to gamble. According to a national survey we did in 1998, three of four Americans who attend religious services regularly (at least once a week) consider casino gaming an acceptable form of entertainment. What is interesting in this survey is that the overwhelming majority of regular churchgoers not only share that attitude, but also are pretty much like the rest of America when it comes to their attitudes and actions about gaming. . . .

Moral questions, of course, cannot be proven or disproved with numbers, research or testimony. But I venture to say that with this widespread acceptability our opponents have a difficult case to make.

Anti-gaming advocates more often rely on the faulty argument that the social costs from gaming exceed the benefits.

They will argue that people go to casinos, lose their money, lose their jobs, end up on welfare or commit crimes, go into bankruptcy and then the public has to pay the price. That reasoning is just not very sound, and is contrary to the facts.

Three Success Stories

In Mississippi, the [casino] industry employs 3 percent of the state's entire work force. Welfare payments have dropped in counties (by as much as 29 percent in the town of Tunica), while most non-casino counties have shown increases.

In Illinois, tax revenues from 10 riverboat casinos reached $236 million in 1995, far exceeding the estimate of $20 million a year made by the Illinois State Legislature before riverboats were legalized. In fact, through October 1996 the boats, which opened in September 1991, have generated a total of $955 million in state and local tax revenues. In Joliet, casinos employ 4,000 people, with an annual payroll of $86 million.

In Louisiana, direct construction expenditures of $574 million over a one-year period created approximately 10,000 construction jobs. This equates to approximately 17 jobs for every $1 million of capital expenditures. In Shreveport, 20 percent of Harrah's casino workers purchased a new home in 1995, 11 percent got off welfare, and 18 percent stopped receiving unemployment payments.

While gaming opponents may offer vague economic theories about gaming revenues, the facts show empirically that when gaming-entertainment is introduced into a region, it creates jobs and generates tax revenues.

American Gaming Association, "Myths and Facts," www.americangaming.org/casino_entertainment/myths_facts/sub_myths.html.

The NGISC made a number of remarkable findings about the positive impact of commercial casinos. The commission makes clear that gambling in the United States is not monolithic and that there are seven very distinct types or classes of gambling with different impacts and benefits on society: 1) commercial casinos; 2) tribal casinos; 3) lotteries; 4) pari-mutuels; 5) charitable gaming; 6) Internet gambling; and 7) illegal gambling.

The commission clearly and unequivocally found that "destination type resorts," such as casinos, offer major economic advantages over what they called "convenience-type gaming," such as non-casino electronic devices or Internet gambling, because they offer quality jobs, economic development and capital investment in their communities. As the report states: "Research conducted on behalf of the commission confirms the testimony of . . . casino workers and government officials that casino gaming creates jobs and reduces the level of unemployment and government assistance in communities that have legalized it."

The report also found that: ". . . Without exception [the elected officials who testified before the commission] expressed support for gambling and recited instances of increased revenues for their cities. They also discussed community improvements made possible since the advent of gambling in their communities and reviewed the general betterment of life for the citizenry in their cities and towns."

The research conducted for the commission backed up those statements. The National Research Council of the National Academy of Sciences (NRC) found that "[g]ambling appears to have net economic benefits for economically depressed communities." Additional research for the commission found that ". . . a new casino of even limited attractiveness, placed in a market that is not already saturated, will yield positive economic benefits on net to its host economy." And the National Opinion Research Center at the University of Chicago (NORC) determined that "[t]hose communities closest to casinos experienced a 12% to 17% drop in welfare payments, unemployment rates and unemployment insurance."

But of course you will not hear about these benefits from industry opponents. You will hear about the so-called social costs, in spite of the facts that came out of the commission report—facts that our opponents like to forget.

Despite documentation to the contrary, opponents continue to recite their "ABCs of gambling"—addiction, bankruptcy and crime. But *let me tell you* what the commission found on these issues.

Starting with the A's . . . On *addiction*, the commission concluded that "[t]he vast majority of Americans either gamble recreationally and experience no measurable side effects related to their gambling, or they choose not to gamble at all. Regrettably, some of them gamble in ways that harm themselves, their families, and their communities." The NORC study conducted for the commission found that the prevalence of problem gambling is approximately 0.1 percent of the U.S. adult population. The NRC study estimated the number at 0.9 percent. A 1997 industry-funded study by Harvard Medical School's Division on Addictions estimated the number at about 1.29 percent. Based on this research, there is a general agreement that approximately 1 percent, or about 2 million people, can be classified as pathological gamblers. That's a far cry from the numbers alleged by opponents of gambling, which we see now had no basis in fact.

But the commission also found that the problem is significant enough to warrant further research. And we agree. When the American Gaming Association was founded in 1995, it was with the commitment that this industry would not repeat the mistakes made by the tobacco industry, by denying the existence of a problem. The vast majority of our customers enjoy gambling as entertainment. The research confirms that. But a small percentage doesn't gamble responsibly. These people deserve our attention and our help, regardless of their numbers.

That's why our segment of the industry, the commercial casino industry, has devoted significant resources to raise awareness of this issue among our employees and customers. We've committed approximately $7 million since 1996 to fund peer-reviewed research on pathological gambling, establishing an independent organization called the National Center for Responsible Gaming. The National Center's organizational structure and decision-making procedures were modeled after the National Institutes of Health to ensure that the highest standards are used to evaluate research grant proposals. The National Center already has awarded more than $3 million in grants to leading researchers at some of the preeminent universities and medical research facilities in the United States and Canada to conduct research in the fields of neuroscience, behavioral social science, with an emphasis on prevention and youth gambling.

The work funded by the National Center has earned the respect of top researchers and scholars. In recognition of that, the grant-making arm of the National Center will now be housed at Harvard Medical School's Division on Addictions, where the newly renamed Institute for Pathological Gambling & Related Disorders will continue to drive the pioneering research we began just four years ago in hopes of furthering our understanding of this disorder and minimizing its impact.

Still on the subject of *addictions*, opponents will argue that increased availability of gambling, access to funds and expanded hours of operation has led to an increase in pathological gambling. While this might seem like a logical assumption to some, it is not valid. The first federal gambling commission during the 1970s found that the number of "probable compulsive gamblers" was 0.77 percent of the U.S. adult population, virtually identical to the findings of the more recent federal commission, despite the growth of gambling opportunities during that time. In addition, research conducted for the 1999 federal commission stated, "The availability of casinos within driving distance does not appear to affect prevalence rates." Similar government-sponsored research in Minnesota, South Dakota and Texas all showed statistically stable rates of pathological gambling in those states, despite increases in the availability of gaming.

Another accusation opponents will make about the industry is that the more people gamble, the more likely they are to become pathological gamblers. Again, all you need to do is look at the commission's research. The NORC report found that while many more people have gambled at least once in their lifetimes (68 percent in 1975, compared to 86 percent in 1999), the number of people who have gambled in the past year has remained relatively unchanged (61 percent in 1975, versus 63 percent in 1999). As Lance deHaven-Smith, executive director of the Public Sector Gaming Study Commission, pointed out in his analysis of the National Gambling Impact Study Commission's final report: "[T]hese findings mean that Americans have become much more likely to have experimented with gambling, but this experimentation has not turned them into people who gamble regularly or routinely."

Gambling opponents also will assert that half of our revenues come from problem and pathological gamblers. In contrast, the NORC report's survey data suggested that between *5 percent and 15 percent* of gaming revenues come from problem and pathological gamblers. Despite this lower percentage, it's important to point out that the industry does not want those with gambling disorders as customers.

Now on to the B's. *There is absolutely no credible evidence establishing a link between bankruptcy and gambling*, although that is one of the industry's opponents' favorite stories. To counter them, you need only look to two independent government studies that failed to find any connection between bankruptcy and gambling. NORC's analysis for the federal commission found that "the casino effect is not statistically significant for . . . bankruptcy. . . ." On top of that, the U.S. Treasury Department investigated this issue and released a report, also in 1999, finding "no connection between state bankruptcy rates and either the extent of or introduction of casino gambling." In preparing its analysis, the Treasury Department examined existing literature on gambling and bankruptcy and conducted new empirical research. According to the study: "Much of the earlier increase in the national bankruptcy rate has been attributed to the changes in the bankruptcy law of 1978. Other economic and social factors cited by researchers as contributing to more recent increases include higher levels of debt relative to income, increasing availability of consumer credit through general purpose credit cards and the reduced social stigma of declaring bankruptcy." This particular study was requested by a leading opponent of gaming in the U.S. Congress after he discovered that the commission's findings were not what he had hoped, costing taxpayers an additional $250,000.

Opponents contend that the economic losses incurred by gambling cause people to commit suicide. As has been demonstrated through recent research by the NRC and Harvard Medical School, individuals who are pathological gamblers often suffer from other disorders; a simplistic approach linking gambling with suicide cannot explain away a decision this complex. While opponents of gambling use anecdotal evidence to attempt to prove a link, recent studies contradict their assumptions. A 1997 report from the Centers for Disease Control (CDC) found that suicide rates are a regional phenomenon and do not mirror the availability of legalized gambling. The CDC study pointed out that suicide levels in the West are 70 percent higher than in the Northeast. A study written for the AGA by a team of researchers from the University of California-Irvine compared actual suicide rates and found that gaming communities have "no higher risk" of suicide than non-gaming communities.

And finally, the C's: opponents' attempts to associate gambling with *crime* and *corruption*. Let's start with their contentions about crime. The federal commission found no link between the two, stating in its research, ". . . the casino effect is not statistically significant for any of the . . . crime outcome measures. . . ." The federal commission's final report also cited a study in which a comprehensive review of publicly available information on gaming and crime found no documentation of a causal relationship between the two.

On the other "C" claim, again, there is no credible evidence other than innuendo suggesting any link between *corruption* and gambling. But the federal commission did make two very important findings related to this. First, they put to rest any notion that there is continued organized crime involvement in the modern casino industry. According to the final report, "All of the evidence presented to the commission indicate that effective state regulation, coupled with the corporate takeover of much of the industry, has eliminated organized crime from the ownership and operation of casinos." The commission also found that "[c]asino gambling, in fact, is the most highly regulated component of the industry." In fact, our industry is one of the most highly regulated in the entire country. Because most of our companies are publicly traded, they come under the stringent scrutiny of the Securities and Exchange Commission (SEC). More than 1,500 regulators and control board members oversee the industry at a total cost of more than $135 million, helping to ensure that only legitimate interests are involved in casino entertainment.

"The positive social and economic impacts of [Indian] gaming . . . far outweigh the negative."

Indian Gaming Benefits Native Americans

Economics Resource Group

In 1998 the Economics Resource Group, Inc. (ERG), a consulting firm, presented a report to the National Gambling Impact Study Commission that summarized ERG's analysis of the economic and social impact of legalized gambling on American Indian reservations. Portions of the report are excerpted below. In them, ERG maintains that Indian gaming has positively impacted American Indian communities by reducing unemployment and increasing revenues to tribal governments. ERG notes that it is unrealistic to expect the revenues from tribal gaming to immediately solve the enormous social and economic problems faced by many American Indian communities. Nevertheless, ERG concludes that, on the whole, tribes that have opened casinos are better off than they were before the spread of Indian casinos.

As you read, consider the following questions:

1. According to ERG, as of 1995, what was the unemployment rate among tribes with Indian games versus those for tribes without?
2. As summarized by the authors, what four purposes does the Indian Gaming Regulatory Act require the revenues from Indian gaming to be used for?
3. Despite the economic success of many Indian casinos, what social problems still plague Native American communities, according to the authors?

Excerpted from *American Indian Gaming Policy and Its Socio-Economic Effects: A Report to the National Gambling Impact Study Commission* by the Economics Resource Group (Cambridge, MA: The Economics Resource Group, July 31, 1998).

Gaming has been a growth industry in Indian Country for nearly two decades. As both the number of gaming tribes and the magnitude of some gaming operations has grown, questions have arisen about gaming's effects. To answer those questions, this study combines an overview of existing studies and available data on Indian gaming generally with a more narrow examination of the impacts of five tribes' gaming operations: the Ho-Chunk Nation (Wisconsin), the Oneida Tribe of Indians of Wisconsin, the Sault Ste. Marie Tribe of Chippewa Indians (Michigan), the Mohegan Tribe (Connecticut), and the Standing Rock Sioux Tribe (North and South Dakota).

Indian Self-Determination and Tribal Casinos

Since late in the nineteenth century, federal policy toward American Indian tribes has repeatedly vacillated between efforts to assimilate individual Indians and break up reservation communities and policies of federal support of various kinds for tribal communities and reservations. These divergent and often conflicting policy approaches have had at least one thing in common: until the late 1970s, all of them failed to ameliorate the crushing poverty and abject social conditions on Indian lands.

This legacy of failed policies stands in stark contrast to the gains made more recently by tribes following the shift to a policy of tribal self-determination. In the mid-1970s the federal government, recognizing in practice the sovereignty tribes already enjoyed in law, began granting to Indian nations enhanced decision-making power over reservation affairs, more complete control over their governments, and more secure property rights to reservation assets. The result has been a dramatic increase in successful, sustained economic development efforts on reservations. In short, the policy of Indian self-determination has been a key to successful reservation development.

Self-determination has found its most controversial expression in the operation of tribal casinos. Like other successful economic activities on Indian reservations, successful Indian gaming is built on tribal sovereignty. The controversy over Indian gaming threatens not only gaming operations themselves, but the self-determination policy that fostered them. Because that policy is the only federal policy in this century that has produced lasting economic benefits for tribes, careful analysis of the consequences of Indian gaming is essential before drawing policy conclusions.

Poor Social Conditions in Indian Country

To fully understand those consequences, we have to answer the counterfactual question: "What would the world have looked like if Indian casinos had not been built?" While the methodological approach to answering this question is exactly the same in relation to Indian gaming as it would be in relation to non-Indian gaming, the legal, economic, and social context in which gaming arose in Indian Country is unique. It is impossible to understand the impact of Indian gaming without a detailed examination of the conditions that prevailed prior to the introduction of casinos.

The available evidence on pre-gaming economic conditions in Indian Country provides a long list of alarming comparisons between tribal economic and social conditions and U.S. national averages: Indian per capita income is about 40% of the national average, the Indian poverty rate is almost four times the national average, the incidence of Indian homes lacking complete plumbing is over 14 times the national average, alcoholism death rates are more than five times the national average for Indian adults and more than 17 times the national average for Indian youths, and so on.

While these nationwide statistics are arresting, our research indicates that the tribes that have opened casinos faced particularly desperate conditions. For example, within a sample of the 75 most populous tribes in the country (as of the 1990 census), 17 of the poorest 20 opened casinos. Furthermore, the group of tribes signing state gaming compacts had higher unemployment in 1989 than their noncompacting counterparts.

The Economic Benefits of Indian Gaming

Against this backdrop of stagnant economies and poor social health, casino gaming has provided an engine for economic growth. It has enabled some tribes to achieve dramatic improvement in such indicators of economic health as employment and income. For example, although tribes that subsequently opened casinos had 24% higher unemployment as a group than non-gaming tribes in 1989, gaming tribes enjoyed 13% lower unemployment than their non-gaming counterparts by 1995. Casino gaming also has enabled some tribes to leverage gaming success into other business success, replacing longstanding dependence on federal assistance with productive, tribally-generated, economic activity.

Tribal Unemployment Pre- and Post-Gaming

Tribe	First Full Yr. of Gaming	Unemployment				
		1987	1989	1991	1993	1995
Wisconsin Winnebago Ho-Chunk	1993	19%	19%	17%	N/A	6%
Oneida	1992	25%	22%	19%	19%	4%
Sault Ste. Marie Chippewa	1992	55%	47%	49%	32%	27%
Standing Rock Sioux	1994	79%	87%	63%	62%	29%

Bureau of Indian Affairs, *Indian Service Population and Labor Force Estimates*, 1987, 1989, 1991, 1993, and 1995.

Improvements in reservation conditions have not been limited to the economic sphere. Tribal gaming is a form of government enterprise (as opposed to private enterprise). Less than 15% of total tribal gaming revenues accrue to non-Indian casino management companies. Tribal governments are obligated by law and by their concern for the well being of tribal members to invest gaming profits in ways that improve tribal welfare. The fruits of these investments are reflected in, among other things, higher graduation rates and lower rates of participation in social assistance programs among members of gaming tribes. These are direct effects of tribal gaming.

Certainly, there have been some negative impacts as well. It seems clear, for example, that the number of compulsive gamblers, both on and off reservations, has grown as Indian gaming has grown. However, this masks the more compelling policy finding: Given the extraordinarily bleak socioeconomic conditions prevalent in Indian Country prior to the introduction of gaming, head counts of compulsive gamblers (even if there were agreement on what constitutes a compulsive gambler) pale in importance beside the demonstrable improvements in social and economic indicators documented for gaming tribes. . . .

In sum, we find that Indian gaming, an expression of Indian self-determination, has produced remarkable movement on stubborn social and economic problems that have been resistant to federal and tribal efforts for decades. While the benefits of gaming are by no means evenly distributed among tribes, a significant number of tribes are making gains economically both through gaming itself and by leveraging gaming revenues into diversified economic activity. Tribes are also translating gaming employment and revenue into significant social change by investing in social and physical infrastructures, thus producing striking improvements in the quality of reservation life. While the legacy of Indian poverty will not be easily erased, and while the vast majority of gaming tribes enjoy only modest gaming income, the economic and social benefits Indian gaming has produced are diverse, substantial, and unprecedented in this century.

Our investigation inescapably yields the conclusion that the positive social and economic impacts of gaming, both on and off reservations, far outweigh the negative. Indeed, for much of Indian Country, the alternative to gaming is the status quo ante: poverty, powerlessness, and despair. Self-determination—and the ways that Indian nations have used it—constitutes a public policy success of major dimensions. Indian gaming is a striking example of that success. . . .

The Social Impact of Indian Gaming

A fully detailed national analysis of Indian gaming's consequences awaits the completion of the next census. However there are a number of preliminary national indicators that hint at the level of impact. This section turns to those indicators.

The most convincing national evidence centers around the question of unemployment. Evidence indicates that tribes sought to go into gaming at the very least to increase tribal employment and that they succeeded at achieving this goal. First, of the 75 most populous reservations in the lower forty-eight states, 17 of the poorest 20 have gaming compacts [agreements with state governments that permit the tribe to operate casinos]. Second, in looking at the period 1989-1996, we find that the tribes that eventually compacted for . . . gaming by 1996 began the period with higher self-reported reservation area unemployment (averaging 41% in 1989) than tribes that did not compact by the end of the period (averaging 33%). Moreover, by 1995, tribes that compacted reported an average of 28% unemployment whereas tribes that did not compact reported 32%. In short, tribes were more likely to compact the more dire their unemployment, and compacting tribes tended to catch up, if not surpass, their non-compacting counterparts in the reduction of unemployment. Thus, for tribal governments gaming represents a very effective policy choice for addressing the backlog of social and economic problems they have inherited from one hundred years' worth of federal experimentation. . . .

Moreover, because Indian gaming is government-sponsored gaming, one would expect there to be focused social spending that would also alleviate poor social conditions. Just as states dedicate lottery revenues to public purposes—e.g., education (California) or natural resource preservation (Minnesota)—so too do tribes. Tribes are required by IGRA [the Indian Gaming Regulatory Act] to expend tribal gaming revenues only: i) to fund tribal government operations or programs; ii) to provide for the general welfare of the Indian tribe and its members; iii) to promote tribal economic development; iv) to donate to charitable organizations; or v) to help fund operations of local government agencies. And, if tribes choose to appropriate some casino net income for per capita payments (the way Alaska allocates oil royalty revenues to its citizens), they must receive Secretarial approval for Gaming Revenue Allocation Plans that specifically apportion the casino net income to the aforementioned categories of expenditure. Even in the absence of the legal impetus to dedicate casino income to social enhancement, tribal governments could not sustainably ignore the dire social conditions on reservations. Federal Indian programs are, by and large, chronically under-funded (see below) and the low levels of educational, health, familial, income, and wealth status indicators for reservation Indians could not be easily ignored by reservation governments—the overwhelming majority of which are elected.

Indian Gaming Is Not a Panacea

What little intercensal social data are available shows a mixed post-gaming picture. As noted, unemployment is in decline by 1995, especially for gaming tribes. Violent crime, however, is currently rising on reservations while declining elsewhere in the country. The Ft. Peck and Navajo reservations, for example, have murder rates that make them on par with the most violent cities in the country. In 1996, Native Americans in non-metropolitan counties were three times as likely as similarly situated non-Hispanic Whites to be below the poverty line and had the highest poverty rate for any ethnic group in the country. In data gathered from 1991 through 1993, Native Americans are shown to be more prone to use and/or abuse alcohol, tobacco, and illegal drugs than almost every other ethnic group.

Finally, the annual Current Population Survey of 1996 shows that the status of rural Indians still lags behind the national average on a number of economic dimensions. . . .

So, while some of the mythology about the "new buffalo" is based on real experience with economic development success, it is important that policy decisions not take Indian social recovery as a foregone conclusion. The vast majority of gaming tribes enjoy modest success or less and the social problems gaming revenues would ameliorate were decades in their creation and are not, in general, likely to accede to a recent increase in tribal wherewithal to remedy them.

VIEWPOINT

"The vast majority of American Indians . . . have not realized the early 'high hopes' of the casino boom."

Indian Gaming Does Not Benefit Most Native Americans

David Pace

David Pace has been a reporter for the Associated Press (AP) since 1978. In the following viewpoint, he summarizes a study the AP conducted in 2000 to determine how the spread of Indian gaming had affected life on Indian reservations. According to Pace, Indian gaming has done very little to lessen the problems of unemployment and poverty on most reservations. The AP study found that the majority of revenues from Indian gaming are concentrated among a few very wealthy tribes. Pace also notes that the majority of tribes do not have casinos, and among tribes that do, only those located near major population centers have been very successful.

As you read, consider the following questions:

1. How many of the 550 federally recognized Indian tribes in the United States does the author say have Las Vegas–style casinos?
2. What was the average rate of unemployment on Indian reservations with established casinos between 1991 and 1997, according to Pace?
3. According to Jacob Coin, the former director of the National Indian Gaming Association, why has the spread of Indian casinos failed to substantially reduce unemployment among American Indians?

When American Indians began embracing gambling as an economic development tool in the 1990s, the Hualapai tribe in northern Arizona moved quickly to open a casino at its Grand Canyon West tourist site.

Tribal leaders figured that slot machines would provide new revenue for the tribe's 1,200 members, many of whom have lived in poverty for years. But they forgot that most of the 100,000 visitors to Grand Canyon West each year come directly from Las Vegas.

"Those people weren't coming to a casino," said Louise Benson, tribal chairman. "They were coming to see the Grand Canyon."

Less than a year after opening the casino, the Hualapai shut it down. Instead of providing an economic boom to tribal members, it left them $1 million in debt.

"There were high hopes for that casino, but the reality of it was that we were too isolated," said Alex Cabillo, the tribe's director of public works.

The Hualapai tribe is one of only two whose casinos failed during the Indian gambling boom of the past decade, when revenues exploded from $100 million in 1988 to $8.26 billion in 1998.

Indian Gaming Has Not Lived Up to Expectations

But an Associated Press computer analysis of federal unemployment, poverty and public assistance records indicates that the vast majority of American Indians, like the Hualapai, have not realized the early "high hopes" of the casino boom.

Two-thirds of the American Indian population belong to poverty-stricken tribes that still don't have Las Vegas–style casinos. Some, like the Navajo, culturally oppose gambling, while others, like the Hualapai, are too far away from major population centers to benefit.

Among the 130 tribes with Las Vegas–style casinos, those near major cities have thrived, while most others have little left after paying the bills, the AP analysis found.

Despite new gambling jobs, unemployment on reservations with established casinos held steady around 54 percent between 1991 and 1997, according to data the tribes reported to the Bureau of Indian Affairs. Many of the casino jobs were filled with non-Indians.

"Everybody thinks that tribes are getting rich from gaming and very few of them are," Benson said.

Of the 500,000 Indians whose tribes operate casinos, only about 80,000 belong to tribes with gambling operations that generate more than $100 million a year.

A Few High-Profile Success Stories

Some of the 23 tribes with the most successful casinos—like the Shakopee Mdewakanton Dakota Tribe in Minnesota—pay each member hundreds of thousands of dollars a year.

In Scott County, which includes the Shakopee reservation south of Minneapolis, the poverty rate declined from 4.1 percent in 1989 to 3.5 percent six years later. The reservation's unemployment rate also plummeted from 70 percent in 1991 to just 4 percent in 1997.

© Asay. Reprinted by permission of Creators Syndicate.

Such success stories belong mostly to tribes with casinos near major population centers.

The tiny Mashantucket Pequot tribe of Connecticut reported more than $300 million in revenue in the first five

125

months of this year from its Foxwoods Casino, located between New York and Boston.

And the Seminole Tribe's Hollywood Gaming Center on Miami's Gold Coast generates more than $100 million a year with pull-tab slot machines. The unemployment rate on that reservation, however, still was 45 percent in 1997, and the average poverty rate in the two counties it touches rose from 10.4 percent in 1989 to 12.1 percent in 1995.

For many tribes with Las Vegas–style casinos, like the San Carlos Apaches in eastern Arizona, gambling revenues pay for casino operations and debt service, with little left to upgrade the quality of life.

Poverty Remains an Enormous Problem

In counties that include reservations with casinos, the average poverty rate declined only slightly between 1989 and 1995, from 17.7 percent to 15.5 percent, the AP analysis found. Counties that include reservations without casinos saw their poverty rate remain steady at slightly more than 18 percent.

Nationally, the poverty rate hovered around 13 percent during the period.

In California, the Tachi Yokut Tribe in the San Joaquin Valley brags on its Web site that its Palace Gaming Center has provided employment for tribal members, helped raise education levels and upgraded housing.

But the poverty rate in Kings County, which includes the tribe's small reservation, climbed from 18.2 percent in 1989 to 22.3 percent in 1995. The reservation's unemployment rate dropped slightly to 49.2 percent in 1997.

Jonathan Taylor, a research fellow at the Harvard University Project on American Indian Economic Development, said many investments gaming tribes have made in social and economic infrastructure don't translate into immediate improvements in quality-of-life indicators like poverty.

"You see investments arising out of gaming taking hold slowly in greater educational success, greater family integrity, greater personal health, greater crime prevention," he said.

There are some optimistic signs that tribes hope to build on as they begin paying off their casino construction loans.

The analysis indicates casino gambling has slowed, though not reversed, the growth of tribal members on public assistance. Participation in the Agriculture Department's Food Distribution Program on Indian Reservations increased 8.2 percent from 1990 to 1997 among tribes with casinos, compared with 57.3 percent among tribes without them.

Unemployment Remains High

And economic development has been spurred in communities near tribal casinos, according to an analysis of the Census Bureau's County Business Patterns for 1990 and 1997.

The Oneida Indian Nation in central New York, for example, has become the largest employer in Oneida and Madison counties, thanks to a casino that's generating more than $100 million in annual revenues. A championship golf course and convention center opened last year.

But overall, the new jobs have not reduced unemployment for Indians. Tribes with established casinos saw their overall unemployment rate actually rise four-tenths of a point to 54.4 percent between 1991 and 1997, the AP analysis found.

Jacob Coin, former executive director of the National Indian Gaming Association, said that's because 75 percent of jobs in tribal casinos are held by non-Indians.

At the Fort Mojave Indian Reservation along the California-Arizona-Nevada border, the unemployment rate climbed from 27.2 percent in 1991 to 74.2 percent in 1997.

Tribal administrator Gary Goforth acknowledged few of the 675 jobs at the tribe's two financially troubled casinos are filled by tribal members. "Not everybody wants to be a dealer, or a housekeeper or even a manager in the restaurant," he said.

Periodical Bibliography

The following articles have been selected to supplement the diverse views presented in this chapter. Addresses are provided for periodicals not indexed in the *Readers' Guide to Periodical Literature*, the *Alternative Press Index*, the *Social Sciences Index*, or the *Index to Legal Periodicals and Books*.

Charlene Bailey	"The Dilemma of Indian Casino Gambling," *Christian Social Action*, April 1999.
Anthony N. Cabot	"Is Legalized Gambling Good Economics for States?" *World & I*, March 1997.
Guy Calvert and Robert E. McCormick	"Gambling and the Good Society—Some Economic Aspects of Gambling," *World & I*, July 2000.
Economist	"Neon in the Delta," September 11, 1999.
Ronald Grover et al.	"Sure There's a Price, But It Pays to Play," *Business Week*, June 21, 1999.
Peter T. Kilborn	"For Poorest Indians, Casinos Aren't Enough," *New York Times*, June 11, 1997.
Jeffrey Klein	"Bad Odds," *Mother Jones*, July/August 1997.
Brad Knickerbocker	"The Growing Costs of Gambling," *Christian Science Monitor*, June 7, 1999.
Anthony Layng	"Indian Casinos: Past Precedents and Future Prospects," *USA Today*, March 1996.
Maclean's	"The Curse of Casinos," May 11, 1998.
Mother Jones	"Heavy Betting," July/August 1997.
Dave Shiflett	"Gambling and Its Discontents," *American Spectator*, March 1999.
Jay Tolson	"The Face of the Future?" *U.S. News &World Report*, cover story on Las Vegas, June 11, 2001.
Jerry Useem	"Bury My Heart at White Clay," *Fortune*, October 2, 2000.
Richard L. Worsnop	"Gambling Under Attack," *CQ Researcher*, September 6, 1996.

CHAPTER 4

How Should the Government Regulate Gambling?

Chapter Preface

"A cultural monster is rapidly smashing old notions of personal and community vice all across America," warns columnist Marianne Means in a 1999 editorial, "the problem is legalized gambling, which used to be widely considered a dangerous sign of moral decline and a flagrant disavowal of the honest virtues of hard work and responsibility." In her column, Means calls on policymakers to do more to halt the spread of legalized gambling.

Means's sentiments echo what economics professor Richard McGowan calls the "ethics of sacrifice." "Those who subscribe to the ethics of sacrifice are asking the public to sublimate the good of the individual to the good of all," he explains. In the case of gambling, critics such as Means believe that policymakers should sacrifice the freedom of individuals to gamble in order to reduce compulsive gambling and thereby benefit society.

Defenders of gambling are more likely to appeal to the "ethics of tolerance," which McGowan sums up with the dictum "you have the right to perform any action as long as that action does not interfere with the rights of others." This view is articulated by Robert R. Detlefsen, a researcher at the libertarian Competitive Enterprise Institute. In response to concerns about compulsive gambling, he writes, "We have alcoholics, shopaholics and workaholics in our midst, and thus far we have not seen fit to ban the activities that cause these maladies. Why should gambling be different? . . . Individuals have an inherent right to spend their time and money on pastimes that do not harm others."

This conflict between the individual and society is at the heart of many social issues. Laws that ban heroin use or require car passengers to wear seatbelts, for example, limit individual freedom for the good of society. In deciding how to regulate gambling, lawmakers must also choose between people's desire to gamble and the risk that problem gambling might harm the community. The authors in the following chapter offer their own perspectives on how the government's policies on gambling might best benefit individuals and society as a whole.

"*Legislators should declare a moratorium on gambling expansion and enact policies to break America's growing addiction to gambling.*"

The Government Should Halt the Spread of Legalized Gambling

Timothy A. Kelly

Timothy A. Kelly is a visiting research fellow at the George Mason Institute for Public Policy. He also served as executive director of the National Gambling Impact Study Commission. In the following viewpoint, Kelly argues that federal, state, local, and tribal governments should work to stop or reverse the spread of legalized gambling in America. Kelly lists the various forms of legalized gambling, such as casino gambling, state lotteries, and sports betting, and discusses what he feels are the harms associated with each. He recommends specific policy initiatives that the government should pursue to reduce gambling, including a ban on college sports betting, increased regulation of gambling advertising, and the passage of a gambling tax, the revenues from which would be used to prevent and treat pathological gambling.

As you read, consider the following questions:

1. How many Native American casinos does the author say there are in the United States?
2. What is a "gray machine," according to Kelly?
3. In Kelly's view, what measures would reduce underage gambling?

Thirty years ago, gambling was illegal in most states and was generally considered to be a vice contrary to the American work ethic. Serious gamblers had to travel to Nevada for casino play; states had not yet plunged into lottery mania. Today, however, 29 casinos operate in Mississippi, 14 in New Jersey, and 429 in Nevada; another 260 casinos operate on Indian reservations; and nearly 100 riverboat casinos are chartered in six states. All but three states have legalized some form of gambling. Pari-mutuel gambling, primarily horseracing, is legal in 42 states; casinos are licensed in 28 states; and the lottery is played in 37 states plus the District of Columbia.

America's Addiction to Gambling

Far from discouraging citizens from risking their hard-earned money on gambling, states spend more than $400 million annually promoting their lotteries with often misleading and deceptive advertising. In fact, more dollars are spent encouraging citizens to gamble than are spent for any other single state message.

Gambling expansion has swept the nation, with 68 percent of the population reporting they have gambled in the past year. They lost an astonishing $50 billion in 1998, and [according to the National Gambling Impact Study Commission] there is "no end in sight: every prediction that the gambling market was becoming saturated has proven to be premature.". . .

But the expansion of gambling carries a high cost. Today, an estimated 15.4 million Americans suffer from problem or pathological gambling, often referred to as gambling addiction. Gambling addiction can be particularly devastating to the individual, his family, and his employer. The National Academies of Science found that "pathological gamblers engage in destructive behaviors: they commit crimes, they run up large debts, they damage relationships with family and friends, and they kill themselves.". . .

How did America become so addicted to gambling? Several factors are clear. First, the lottery states have given a powerfully motivating message to their citizens by declaring that gambling is not only acceptable, but actually the right thing to do because it increases state revenue for good causes. Second, the Indian Gaming Regulatory Act of 1988 opened the floodgate for Native American casinos, which are expanding more rapidly now than any other form of gambling. Third, legislators at the state and federal levels have acted without the benefit of objective information on the full costs and benefits of gambling operations, since nearly all of the previous impact studies have been sponsored by the gambling industry. The Gambling Commission report provides the most comprehensive and objective evaluation of gambling impacts to date. But more research is needed if policymakers are to understand fully the likely consequences before moving ahead with gambling expansion initiatives.

The Gambling Commission report, which was unanimously adopted, calls for a moratorium on gambling expansion. This is especially noteworthy because four of the nine commissioners represented or endorsed gambling industry interests. The purpose of the moratorium: to allow policymakers to review what has already been approved and to demand better cost/benefit analyses before moving ahead with any new initiatives.

More than a moratorium, however, will be needed if America is going to manage gambling for the public good as opposed to the public treasury. The Gambling Commission report included 77 far-reaching recommendations, all of which are worthy of consideration. Eight policy recommendations, based upon but not identical to the Commission's recommendations, should constitute a priority for federal and state/tribal legislators. Legislative action based on these recommendations would jump-start America's recovery from its addiction to gambling. Before discussing these recommendations in detail, however, a review of the seven major types of legalized gambling reveals the gravity of the current problem.

Legalized Gambling in America

Seven major forms of gambling are legal in America today, each presenting a different array of costs and benefits, and each raising a unique set of issues that must be addressed by policymakers.

Commercial casinos. Commercial casinos (land casinos not owned by Native Americans)—with their table games and slot machines—symbolize the gambling industry for most Americans. Until this decade, casinos were legal only in Nevada and Atlantic City, but during the past 10 years they have expanded into 28 states. In 1997, commercial casinos took in $26.3 billion in revenue. Destination casinos (those with large hotels) provide an important source of jobs, tax revenue, and entertainment for their localities. Many customers enjoy the associated food, entertainment, and conference facilities.

At the same time, there are costs associated with commercial casinos. The 15.4 million pathological and problem gamblers account for a significant portion of gambling revenues. They often end up hurting not only themselves but also family, friends, and business partners. Direct costs from their bankruptcies, arrests, imprisonments, legal fees for divorce, and so on come to more than $5 billion each year. Who should be responsible for these costs and liabilities?

A less visible but perhaps more insidious cost involves the political clout that commercial casino interests inevitably develop. Given the vast revenue generated by successful casinos, it becomes increasingly difficult for other voices to be heard in the political process. For instance, non-gambling retailers and restaurant owners may find that their customer base dwindles after the introduction of casinos and that local government turns a deaf ear to their complaints. In fact, once gambling enters a community, local government tends to become [according to the Gambling Commission report] "a dependent partner in the business of gambling."

Native American casinos. Large-scale Indian casino gambling began in the late 1980s. In 1988, Congress passed the Indian Gaming Regulatory Act (IGRA), which set the stage for a rapid expansion of Native American casinos—now numbering about 260. IGRA called for the states and tribes to enter into compacts allowing casinos on Indian reservations to offer whatever form of gambling is legal in the state. It also called for gambling revenue to be used to promote the economic development and welfare of the tribe. Thus, revenues are not subject to state or federal taxation, but are to be used as an economic engine to address tribal needs. In

1997, Indian casinos generated $6.7 billion in revenue from gambling, much of which went to improve the health, education, and welfare of the casino tribes.

Problem and pathological gambling among tribal members and their customers is, of course, as much a concern here as it is for non-tribal casinos. Concerns also have been raised about the adequacy of Indian casino regulations and the distribution of funds among the tribes that own casinos versus the majority that do not. Furthermore, some states and tribes have not been able to agree on compacts that suit both sides. All of these issues need to be resolved, perhaps within the context of IGRA revisions and amendments.

Riverboat casinos. Riverboat casinos are a new phenomenon, having begun in Iowa in 1991 as a means for tourism and economic development. Most of these casinos do not actually sail out on the rivers, but are simply built over water as part of zoning requirements. In 1997, riverboat casinos brought in $6.1 billion in revenue from gambling.

Often built deliberately on the borders shared with other states, these casinos initially brought significant additional tax revenues from the citizens of neighboring states. Eventually, however, the adjoining states ended up building their own casinos to recapture the lost revenue. Once the saturation point has been reached by neighboring states, whether the economic benefits outweigh the social costs is not clear. However, for this reason Iowa recently legislated a five-year moratorium on casino expansion in order to better assess the full impacts of gambling. Such a moratorium is precisely what the Gambling Commission recommended for all gambling states.

The Spread of Lottery Gambling

State lotteries. Colonial America used lotteries to help fund public works such as paving streets; since that time, there has been a cyclical aspect to their usage. In the 1870s, gambling scandals involving the bribery of state and federal officials led to lotteries being outlawed altogether, along with most forms of gambling. The current lottery revival began in 1964 with the New Hampshire lottery; today, 37 states and the District of Columbia have lotteries.

Modern lotteries offer an array of products, including instant scratch-off tickets, daily numbers drawings, weekly Lotto and Powerball drawings, and video keno, which involves multiple drawings per hour. In 1997, U.S. lotteries produced $16.5 billion in revenue from tickets and other sales. This revenue is used to add to the public treasury to address education and/or other needs.

The Gambling Commission contracted with national lottery experts, Drs. Cook and Clotfelter from Duke University, to research the impacts of state-sponsored lottery gambling. They documented conclusively that lotteries function as a regressive tax, taking from the poor and giving to those better off. As Cook stated, "It's astonishingly regressive. The tax that is built into the lottery is the most regressive tax we know." Those making less than $10,000 per year spend more than any other income group, averaging $597 per year. Furthermore, the top 5 percent of lottery players account for over 50 percent of lottery sales, spending on average $3,870 per year.

A review of marketing strategies revealed that states advertise in low-income neighborhoods, which tend to be saturated with lottery outlets. They use ads that are "misleading, even deceptive" [according to the Gambling Commission report]. Such ads are exempt from the Federal Trade Commission's truth-in-advertising standards since they come from state governments.

Another concern is the ease with which minors can participate in lottery gambling, despite legal restrictions. For instance, a Massachusetts survey found that minors as young as nine years of age were able to purchase lottery tickets on 80 percent of their attempts, and that 75 percent of the high school seniors reported playing the lottery. Such experiences can function as a gateway to more intensive gambling and to pathological gambling.

All of this raises the fundamental question of whether states should even be in the lottery business in the first place, spending hundreds of millions of dollars each year encouraging citizens—including those who can least afford it—to gamble their money away in order to feed the state treasury. A growing number of people, such as those citizens who recently rejected a lottery referendum in Alabama, answer "no." The role of the state is to provide for the public good, not to feed the public treasury at any cost.

Racetracks and Sports Betting

Pari-mutuel wagering. Pari-mutuel gambling consists primarily of horseracing, but includes greyhound racing and jai alai. The term pari-mutuel connotes the fact that wagers are put into a common pool, with the odds dependent on the total amount bet on any given horse. Legal in 43 states, several of the major racetracks have been in operation since the 1800s. Total revenue in 1997 amounted to $3.25 billion. Unique to this form of gambling, the horseracing industry supports a thriving agro-industrial economic sector of trainers, owners, breeders, and stable owners. Although more than 150 racetracks are licensed, most betting takes place through off-track sites or, more recently, through cable and Internet broadcasts directly into the home.

A major policy issue has been raised by those tracks that

have attempted to add casino-like gambling devices such as slot machines to their facilities in order to increase revenue. This, in effect, creates a "mini-casino" in an area that was not necessarily zoned for casinos. Additionally, concerns have been raised about the advisability of beaming pari-mutuel gambling into homes via cable and Internet, where children may participate.

Sports wagering. Sports wagering is illegal in all but two states, Nevada and Oregon, but is nonetheless popular in homes and offices. Oregon only allows lottery players to include a wager on pro football games. Nevada, on the other hand, has 142 legal sports books for wagering on just about any prediction for professional or amateur sports events. These books took in $77.4 million in 1997. However, Americans wager an estimated $80 billion each year on illegal sports betting, usually without realizing its illegality.

One reason that sports wagering is so widespread is the easy availability of the Las Vegas "line," or point spread, published in newspapers across the country. Although some claim that the line increases sports interest, it more likely simply increases sports wagering.

Perhaps the worst effect of sports wagering is its impact on youth and college students. The National College Athletics Association points out that sports wagering seriously threatens the integrity of college sports and puts student-athletes at considerable risk. There are student bookies on most campuses, organized crime is often involved, and consequences can be tragic—including suicide over an unpaid gambling debt. A recent study found that more than 5 percent of male student-athletes had provided inside information for gambling purposes, bet on a game in which they participated, or accepted money for performing poorly in a game. Furthermore, sports wagering can function as a gateway to other forms of gambling and to pathological gambling.

The Dangers of Internet Gambling

Internet gambling. First appearing in 1995, Internet gambling is the newest form of gambling. Today hundreds of on-line casinos, lotteries, and sports books are advertised on mainline Web sites. With a credit card number, customers can play a video version of blackjack, slot machines, poker, roulette, or other games. One study showed that Internet gambling revenues doubled in only one year, from $445.4 million in 1997 to $919.1 million in 1998. Some countries, such as Australia and Antigua, have licensed Internet gambling operators within their borders. Their products are, of course, accessible by anyone, anytime, anywhere, via the Internet.

Internet gambling, like Internet pornography, has been perceived as a threat to children and adolescents precisely because it is so easily available in the home and in college dorms. No one uses the Internet more than America's youth, and no one is more vulnerable to its temptations. Now, every parent has to reckon with the fact that commercial gambling is available in the dens and bedrooms of their homes via the Internet.

Internet gambling can be especially destructive for those who are vulnerable to addictions, since it provides high-speed instant gratification together with the anonymity of the home setting. A Harvard researcher stated, "As smoking crack cocaine changed the cocaine experience, I think electronics is going to change the way gambling is experienced." In other words, electronic gambling is all the more destructive and addictive.

For these and other reasons, including crime and fraud potential, many policymakers are calling for the outright prohibition of Internet gambling. Several states have passed legislation to that effect, and Congress is considering a bill, introduced by Senator Jon Kyl (R-Ariz.), titled "The Internet Gambling Prohibition Act." [As of summer 2001, this legislation has not passed.] Furthermore, the National Association of Attorneys General has called for the federal government to prohibit Internet gambling, recognizing that the issue cannot be resolved on the state level. The Gambling Commission, as well, recommended prohibiting Internet gambling outright. However, given the difficulty inherent in restricting commerce of any kind, whether Internet gambling will be stopped is not clear.

Convenience gambling. Convenience gambling refers to gambling machines that have proliferated in communities and neighborhood areas such as convenience stores, truck stops, and bars. These stand-alone machines, which include video poker, video keno, and slot machines, are known as Electronic Gambling Devices, or EGDs. Some states, such as South Carolina, allow EGDs to operate just about anywhere on a 24-hour basis. In other states, EGDs are run by the state lottery. In Nevada, EGDs can be found in the airport, in supermarkets, in sandwich shops, and elsewhere. Many states also have quasi-legal EGDs known as "gray machines" that are not licensed to pay out winnings and are, supposedly, for amusement only. In reality, winnings are often paid out surreptitiously.

Convenience gambling in some ways represents gambling at its worst. Since EGDs can be almost anywhere, avoiding them is difficult. In some Las Vegas neighborhoods, for instance, a resident cannot even buy a gallon of milk without walking past rows of gambling machines. This makes it much more difficult for those who are vulnerable to addictions to avoid playing and significantly increases the incidence of problem and pathological gambling. For instance, South Carolina, with over 34,000 EGDs, is experiencing a surge of problem and pathological gambling.

Furthermore, this is one more form of gambling that is particularly detrimental to children and adolescents, as it presents them with numerous opportunities to become introduced to gambling experiences at an early age. Many of them will develop into problem and pathological gamblers, having been put at risk for the sake of America's appetite for gambling.

At the same time, economic benefits to the public treasury are minimized since it is usually the local owner—not the state—who collects the lion's share of profits. For these reasons, the Gambling Commission recommended not only that states no longer approve convenience gambling, but also that they roll back existing operations. This is precisely what happened in South Carolina, where a recent court decision will likely lead to the removal of that state's 34,000 EGDs.

Federal Policy Recommendations

Since most gambling laws and regulations are established at the state or tribal level, it is primarily up to policymakers at these levels to take the lead in responding to the tough issues raised by gambling expansion. However, a few areas require federal action. Policy recommendations for the 106th Congress that, if enacted, would greatly support state and tribal efforts to control gambling expansion, include the following:

• Ban betting on collegiate and amateur athletic events altogether, and prohibit media from advertising the line on those events. Sports wagering, especially on collegiate and other amateur events, undermines the integrity of sports and puts students and athletes at risk. It should be prohibited where currently legal; where illegal, regulations should be more rigorously enforced. Newspapers should be prohibited from printing point spreads for athletic contests in areas where sports wagering is illegal.

• Amend truth-in-advertising laws to apply to Native American and state lottery gambling ads. Many lottery ads have been found to be misleading or deceptive; truth-in-advertising laws currently do not apply to states or tribal entities.

• Prohibit Internet gambling not already authorized and develop enforcement strategies. Help foreign governments to prohibit Internet gambling that preys on U.S. citizens. Because of the dangers posed by Internet gambling—especially to America's families and their children and adolescents who are put at risk—Internet gambling sites should be prohibited.

State/Tribal Policy Recommendations

Because state and tribal policymakers set most of the nation's gambling laws and regulations, they carry the heaviest burden for assuring that those laws are crafted in the interest of the public good. Following are policy recommendations for state and tribal leaders that would not only go a long way towards reigning in uncontrolled gambling expansion, but also would begin to address costs associated with it:

• Restrict contributions to state and local campaigns from corporate, private, or tribal entities operating gambling facilities in that state. Because campaign contributions by gambling interests may unduly influence the political process and because local government tends to become a dependent partner in the business of gambling, states should adopt tight restrictions on contributions to state and local campaigns by entities—corporate, private, or tribal—that have applied for, or have been granted, the privilege of operating gambling facilities.

• Prohibit convenience gambling (casino-like machines and games) in neighborhoods, pari-mutuel facilities, and lottery terminals. Convenience gambling, such as EGDs in neighborhood outlets, has been shown to provide little to no social or economic benefit, and to contribute to significant negative costs.

• Detach state government from the operation and promotion of lotteries. Lottery states cannot avoid a conflict of interest between the public good and the public treasury. They are actively promoting an addictive product that functions like a regressive tax and that is essentially contrary to the work ethic on which viable democracy is based.

• Enact and enforce harsh penalties for any gambling outlet that allows underage gambling. America's growing addiction to gambling puts children and adolescents at considerable risk for gambling addiction through early and repeated exposure. State and tribal leaders should enact and enforce harsh penalties for any abuses regarding allowing or encouraging underage gambling. Penalties and enforcement efforts should be greatly increased.

• Establish a 1 percent gambling addiction tax on all gambling operations dedicated to providing research, prevention, education, and treatment for problem and pathological gamblers. The social costs inherent in legalized gambling, including problem and pathological gambling and its consequences, have not been adequately addressed.

The Courage to Act

The Gambling Commission report stated:

> Gambling, like any other viable business, creates both profits and jobs. But the real question—the reason gambling is in need of substantially more study—is not simply how many people work in the industry, nor how much they earn, nor even what tax revenues flow from gambling. The central issue is whether the net increases in income and well-being are worth the acknowledged social costs of gambling.

Because the costs are high, especially for America's youth, a moratorium on gambling expansion is needed now. . . .

It is time for policymakers to recognize that the rapid expansion of gambling is putting children and adolescents increasingly at risk and has led to a host of other negative social consequences that have yet to be adequately addressed. Legislators should declare a moratorium on gambling expansion and enact policies to break America's growing addiction to gambling. They must reach out to the many broken lives that have resulted from gambling addiction on a personal level and take action to prevent America's youth from falling prey to gambling's destructive potential. The above policy recommendations will jump-start that process, but the Gambling Commission's Final Report should also be consulted for additional resource data and information.

The question is not so much what can be done—there are many ways to begin, as these recommendations illustrate. The real question is: Do policymakers have the courage to act on behalf of the public good, as opposed to the public treasury?

> "*A more paternalistic government policy [toward gambling] would . . . make a mockery of any doctrine of individual responsibility.*"

The Government Should Respect Individuals' Freedom to Gamble

Guy Calvert

In the following viewpoint, Guy Calvert maintains that government efforts to restrict gambling do more harm than good. Calvert believes that many of the arguments against gambling—such as the growing prevalence of pathological gambling—are exaggerated. Furthermore, he maintains that individuals should not be prohibited from gambling just because some people find it addictive. Finally, he warns that the dangers of prohibiting gambling outweigh the benefits, citing the prohibition of alcohol in the 1920s as an example. Guy Calvert is a quantitative analyst at a Wall Street firm.

As you read, consider the following questions:
1. According to the study cited by Calvert, how much higher is the average income of casino players, as compared to the general U.S. population?
2. Why does the author feel that compulsive gamblers should not be forced into self-help programs like Gamblers Anonymous?
3. What quote by philosopher John Stuart Mill does Calvert cite in support of his argument?

Excerpted from "Gambling America: Balancing the Risks of Gambling and Its Regulation," by Guy Calvert, *Cato Policy Analysis*, June 18, 1999. Copyright © 1999 by the Cato Institute. Reprinted with permission.

Along with smoking, drinking, and skiing without a helmet, gambling is once again under the microscope. In 1996 Congress established the National Gambling Impact Study Commission to "conduct a comprehensive study of the social and economic impacts of gambling in the United States." But instead of making a "comprehensive study," the NGISC has confined itself to a fairly narrow review. In particular, the commission's research agenda declares a determination to get to the bottom of "problem and pathological gambling." That is fine as far as it goes, but in view of the constant pressure for government intervention, any study of the impact of gambling should consider the impact of gambling regulation as well.

And pressure there is. Outraged moralists, fretting about a supposed threat to public virtue and fed up with the states' liberal attitude toward gambling, have elevated their campaign to the federal level and expect action. Their goal [according to researchers William A. Galston and David Wasserman]: "a strategy of containment to minimize the moral risks of gambling for individuals and society."

The charge of "moral risk" conjures up a grim portrait of parents' abandoning their familial responsibilities in favor of uncontrollable gambling, soaking up welfare dollars, and then unleashing their disaffected children to wreak havoc on the community. But in view of the available evidence, some of which is reviewed below, such charges are overblown. The overriding risk—to both individuals and society—is that harsh government measures intended to control or suppress gambling will simply usher in a new era of public corruption, compromising the integrity of government officials, judges, and the police. And for all of that, such measures would do next to nothing to deter truly compulsive gamblers from gambling.

Government-Imposed Restrictions Are Unnecessary

Moreover, a government "strategy of containment" is clearly unnecessary to prevent force or fraud in dealings between gamblers and casinos, bookmakers, and others. All that is required is the rigorous enforcement of contracts, together with an effort by vendors to acquire third-party accreditation of the integrity of their games. A more paternalistic government policy would, quite apart from intruding on the liberties of gamblers and others, make a mockery of any doctrine of individual responsibility—hardly the best way to sustain the moral health of the nation.

Not even, for that matter, the economic health. In case the point has escaped notice, the nation is not in a gambling-induced slump. On the contrary, just as the gambling industry has for the last few years grown rapidly, the American economy has all the while enjoyed heady times. And the gambling boom continues today. While an overwhelming majority of states enthusiastically promote homegrown lotteries, interest in casino gaming is flourishing. According to a recent Harrah's survey, fully 32 percent of U.S. households gambled at a casino in 1996. Those who did averaged 4.8 visits, for an overall total of 176 million visits. And this figure is up 14 percent from 1995. America, it seems, has found a new pastime, or rediscovered an old one.

Gambling, ever dogged by controversy, has a long and colorful history. Historians Lisa Morris and Alan Block hold that "until the 1840s professional, organized gambling was primarily carried out on steamboats plying the Mississippi and Ohio Rivers and the Great Lakes." Later, in spite of prohibition—or perhaps because of it—underworld gambling operations thrived on land, spawning "a series of infamous 'crime towns.'" Lotteries, moreover, hark back to the Old World; Queen Elizabeth chartered the first English lottery, which was drawn in 1569. Later, in both colonial America and the independent United States, lotteries prospered as a much-promoted and voluntary means of supplementing the public coffers. But a steady procession of public scandals took its toll, and in the 19th century a political backlash against lotteries culminated in universal prohibition. The legal lottery did not return until 1963 in New Hampshire; between 1965 and 1993, 35 states and the District of Columbia introduced state lottery monopolies. And so the historical tug-of-war between gambling proponents and detractors continues.

The lesson of history is clear. For all the moralists' bluster, the evident predilection of the American people to gamble is unique neither to modern times nor, indeed, to Americans. To all appearances it is inextricably bound up with the propensity of human beings to take risks, an enduring and arguably benign trait of our nature. Granted, people enjoy gambling for many reasons, some of which may well seem unfathomable to other people. But there is common ground too. For to gamble, by definition, is to play games of chance for money. At heart, therefore, gambling is a combination of risk and ritual. Both components are mainstays of human society, for the very good reason that they are a part of our makeup. It is no wonder, therefore, that gambling is universal.

I do not suggest here that gambling behavior, simply because it is natural, is necessarily a moral good. For in many ways the morality issue is beside the point—if gambling is a vice then that is a matter for philosophers or the clergy, and ultimately individual conscience. My main concern is that a coercive effort to eliminate or reduce gambling must compete against that most formidable opponent, human nature. And in any case, gambling is hardly such a danger as to merit heavy-handed intervention. Indeed, in moderation there is much to be said for it: at the very least gambling, for many people, can be fun. Moreover, gambling games, insofar as players must balance risk and reward, offer the opportunity to develop a widely applicable set of skills. In the marketplace and the poker room alike, it pays to know when to hold 'em and when to fold 'em.

The Case Against Gambling

While many Americans have embraced the growing opportunities to wager, the critics of gambling have been vocal in their dissent. The various state lotteries are almost universally denounced as immoral and economically harmful. While state revenue hawks undoubtedly enjoy the rake (proceeds), critics [such as Galston and Wasserman] argue that "losses fall disproportionately on some of the more vulnerable members of society." Meanwhile, casinos are accused of displacing—even "cannibalizing"—rival service and entertainment businesses, such as hotels, restaurants, and theme parks. Worse, it is alleged, this is achieved by ruthlessly exploiting the addictions of compulsive gamblers, thereby causing financial distress, destabilizing families, and fueling welfare dependence and crime.

Viewed in context, those charges lack merit. To begin with, many of the crime statistics underlying the "gambling breeds crime" hypothesis have been hotly contested on the grounds of dubious measurement techniques. For example, early analysis of Atlantic City crime figures shortly after the arrival of casinos suggested that per capita crime had markedly increased. However, the per capita crime statistics failed to take account of the swelling of the local population due to casino-related tourism, so the estimates of crime were inflated. When the crime statistics for Atlantic City were readjusted to take account of this and other elementary crime-reporting errors, the resulting crime levels were unremarkable.

Most People Gamble Responsibly

At a more fundamental level, there is no evidence that gamblers are any more likely than nongamblers to forsake responsibility. Indeed, one Swedish study found no relationship between gambling and crime, marital instability, or "the degree of participation in community activities." In another survey, the economist Reuven Brenner of McGill University notes that there is "little evidence to support the view that the majority of gamblers squander their money recklessly, whether it is money spent on stakes or money earned from winnings."

> There is evidence that many people budget for their expenditures, that participants intend to use any large win thriftily and sensibly and in fact do so, spending the money by preference on home-centered items if and when they win.

It is certainly true that the lottery appeals mostly to older people or those of lesser means. In view of the embarrassingly high rake, those who defend the states' monopolies against the forces of competition have a difficult case to answer. But insofar as casino gaming is concerned, the crucial point is that if gamblers are being exploited, they are no worse off for it. Indeed, people who gamble in casinos are not crazed, welfare-dependent casino desperados; they are (by contrast with lottery players) in many respects better off than the average American. A recent industry study found that while the "median age of casino players is similar to that of the U.S. population" (about 48 years), they have more schooling—they are more likely to have done some college and more likely also to have graduated from college. Moreover, the average household income of casino players is 28 percent higher than that of the U.S. population. The details are reproduced in Table 1. Demographics aside, the behavioral portrait of a gambler is striking. An earlier Federal Gambling Commission report declared that gamblers "watch somewhat less television than nongamblers, read more newspapers and magazines, and read about as many books."

> Gamblers devote more time to opera, lectures, museums, nightclubs, dancing, movies, theater and active sports. They also socialize more with friends and relatives and participate more in community activities.

In other words, instead of withdrawing from civil society, the typical gambler appears to embrace it wholeheartedly.

Compulsive Gamblers

Yet horror stories of compulsive gambling grab the headlines. Indeed, it is no accident that these issues drive the agenda of the NGISC. While that is understandable, it is hardly the most reliable starting point for gambling policy.

Nobody denies that there are those who, for whatever reason, gamble in ways that harm themselves and others. But while the severe cases are thought to be uncommon, it is difficult to say much more. Measurement and classification problems haunt efforts to reliably estimate prevalence. As if to underline the confusion, William Galston and David Wasserman, in their celebrated moral critique of gambling, concede:

> Although several studies have found large increases in compulsive and problem gambling following the introduction of state lotteries or casinos, the reliability of these findings is limited by inconsistency and vagueness in the definition of "compulsive" and "problem" gambling and by the possibility that much of the apparent increase is due to increased awareness and increased reporting.

And limited also by the difficulty of pinning down the sources. None of the "several studies" they mention here are actually cited by Galston and Wasserman, and in fact other studies seem to show no such increase. For example, a study of gambling behavior in Connecticut found that "probable pathological gambling rates may actually have fallen . . . and have certainly not risen, during a period [1991–96] in which one of the largest casinos in the world was opened in the state."

Table 1: Profile of Casino Gamblers

	Traditional Destination Player Profile	New Destination Player Profile	United States Population
Median household income	$44,000	$39,000	$32,000
Male/female ratio	52/48	50/50	49/51
Median age	49	47	48
Education			
No college	48%	50%	51%
Some college	23%	22%	22%
College graduate	19%	18%	17%
Postgraduate	10%	9%	10%
Employment			
White collar	43%	41%	41%
Blue collar	27%	29%	28%
Retired	16%	16%	16%
Other	14%	14%	15%

Harrah's Survey of Casino Entertainment, using data from NFO Research and the Bureau of the Census, www.harrahs.com/survey/ce97/ce97_demographics.html.

Note: A "traditional" destination is a casino in Nevada or New Jersey. A "new" destination is an Indian or other casino.

Moreover, to the extent that compulsive gamblers behave badly toward others, it is not always due to gambling. Another detractor of gambling, Ronald A. Reno, figures that "1 to 3 percent of the adult population are pathological gamblers" but notes that "about half of compulsive gamblers experience problems with alcohol and substance abuse." That is quite a confounding factor: abuse of alcohol alone is associated with all manner of disorderly behavior. In 1996 alcohol was involved in 40.9 percent of road fatalities and was perceived to be a factor by three-fourths of the victims of spousal violence.

This is not to belittle the tribulations of compulsive gamblers or their relations. Truly pathological gambling can and sometimes does result in genuine human misery. But the same—or worse—is true of alcohol abuse, and yet we recognize that alcoholism is best addressed on a voluntary basis rather than through prohibition. Likewise, the best recourse for compulsive gamblers would appear to be counseling and abstinence, not government intervention to prohibit or otherwise limit gambling; after all, compulsive gamblers were probably regular clientele of the many illegal casinos and "bust-out joints" that preceded gambling legalization. And voluntary self-help programs such as Gamblers Anonymous, to have any effect, must truly be voluntary. As the GA literature makes clear, the "compulsive gambler needs to be willing to accept the fact that he or she is in the grip of a progressive illness and has a desire to get well. Our experience has shown that the Gamblers Anonymous program will . . . never work for the person who will not face squarely the facts about this illness." GA also insists on financial independence. Declining any "outside contribution . . . expenses are met through voluntary financial support by the members." Government assistance, it seems, is not welcome.

Irrational Exuberance

In all, the compulsive gambling brouhaha serves mainly to prop up the other charge often leveled by casino critics—that casinos unjustly displace other businesses. True, if people overwhelmingly prefer gambling to other sources of entertainment, some existing businesses may not be able to compete effectively. But this alleged substitution effect is both overstated and quite beside the point. For this is really a matter of consumer taste rather than justice and is certainly a weak excuse for government involvement. Should government protect nongambling businesses from competition in the name of protecting a few compulsive gamblers from themselves? Those businesses might well think so, but in view of their evident conflict of interest, it is a tough argument to make. One cannot help but be suspicious. The trick, therefore, is to portray gambling as primarily a public health issue, which just incidentally threatens the viability of rival businesses. Perhaps all gamblers, not just a compulsive minority, are sick.

The argument turns on the persistent belief that gambling is something entirely irrational. That perception often underpins the moral case against casinos and lotteries alike, for here the gambler squares off against a formidable enemy—the laws of probability. As [author] Mario Puzo's fictional casino president, Gronevelt, asserts colorfully: "Percentages never lie. We built all these hotels on percentages. We stay rich on the percentage."

That shocking revelation, that casinos look to make money from gamblers, is of course true. If it were any other way, the shareholders would have none of it. But it is absurd to confuse the purposes of casinos with those of their patrons, or to pretend that those very patrons are a homogeneous group who all want the same thing and behave in the same way.

In the first place, for some gamblers the "percentage" runs quite the other way. Shrewd poker players rightly expect to make money in the long run. And for those who clandestinely count at blackjack, the odds are typically 1 percent or so in their favor, depending on the particular house rules, counting system used, and skill of the counter. Indeed, this fact may explain why blackjack (or 21) is perhaps the most popular table game in casinos.

More important is the entertainment value of gambling—it is not merely semantics to talk of the "gaming industry." Gamblers may sometimes gamble simply for the exhilaration of a night out under the casino lights. Part of the thrill, no doubt, derives from the very real prospect of winning money, and from taking a risk. Gambling also allows us to control the amount of risk we expose ourselves to; we rarely get to "play" with risk like that in real life, at least not at such low stakes. In any case, to ignore the entertainment value of gambling is a little like ignoring the exercise value of jogging.

It is worth reflecting on this point in detail. For the willingness to pay significant sums for entertainment alone is hardly unique to gamblers: sports fans, for example, are apt to spend several hundred dollars a year on stadium tickets, and opera aficionados routinely shell out even more. This kind of behavior is rightly embraced as a healthy and vigorous celebration of our culture, even as gambling is characterized as a widespread compulsive disorder. . . .

The Perils of Prohibition

Those detractors of gambling contemplating a federal "strategy of containment" would do well to note the similarity between their position and that of the early temperance reformers. For, as economist Mark Thornton explains, the "noble experiment" was an unmitigated disaster:

> Although consumption of alcohol fell at the beginning of Prohibition, it subsequently increased. Alcohol became more dangerous to consume; crime increased and became "organized"; the court and prison systems were stretched to the breaking point; and corruption of public officials was rampant. No measurable gains were made in productivity or reduced absenteeism. Prohibition removed a significant source of tax revenue and greatly increased government spending. It led many drinkers to switch to opium, marijuana, patent medicines, cocaine, and other dangerous substances that they would have been unlikely to encounter in the absence of Prohibition.

It is essential to note that while the particulars of this experience derive from the circumstances of the time, the generalities follow a pattern that should be familiar to economists. Prohibitionist policies impose costs in several ways.

Of course, there is an immediate loss of liberty inasmuch as consumption of the good or service in question is now prohibited by law. This cost is incurred not only by those directly affected (the would-be producers and consumers) but also by those who value personal freedom generally and mourn the loss of liberty itself. Similarly, we are all penalized if effective enforcement of the prohibition leads to the erosion of certain legal rights or liberties, such as an easement of constraints on evidence gathering by police, probable cause for search and seizure on private property, and so on.

Moreover, there are the direct costs of enforcement to the taxpayer, who must now either foot the bill for additional police or put up with a lower level of police service elsewhere due to redirection of existing police resources. And taxpayers are further shortchanged to the extent that the justice system for which they pay is infiltrated with public officials, such as lawmakers, judges, and police officers, who have been corrupted by the rewards of trade in contraband.

In addition, and increasing with the enforcement costs, there are the evasion costs imposed on the not-so-easily-dissuaded consumer of the prohibited good or service. Those costs are particularly significant if the good or service in question admits a class of "compulsive consumers," who for whatever reason just cannot kick the habit (examples include gambling and also prostitution, tobacco, alcohol, and some other drugs). To the extent that the prohibition law was initially passed in a paternalistic effort to protect compulsive consumers from themselves, those costs are somewhat perverse.

Of course, the more widespread the prohibition, the greater the costs. Insofar as gambling is concerned, a statewide prohibition is hardly as bad as a federal prohibition, since in the former case one is free to pursue gambling activities in other jurisdictions. For example, a gambler from Connecticut can always head to Las Vegas or Atlantic City for a weekend of unrestricted casino gaming (or perhaps drive a couple of hours to an Indian casino in her own state). But even then, extra costs are incurred in travel, lost time, and so forth, all of which amount to a deadweight loss.

Another point is that a few, isolated centers of legal gambling will nevertheless attract the entire population of truly compulsive, hard-core gamblers—those few who, by definition, would incur almost any cost rather than stop gambling. It follows that the number of compulsive gamblers in each casino will typically be disproportionately high compared with the general population. So while the casual casino tourist could sometimes be forgiven for believing that "casinos corrupt the local community," that impression is clearly a distortion, and one that a broader prohibition will tend to exaggerate all the more. . . .

The public conflict over gambling animates a larger debate that is of crucial importance to all Americans. On one side is the view that, in some situations, individuals cannot be trusted to face the personal consequences of their own decisions, and so cannot be held accountable when things go wrong. Therefore, in the public interest, government officials must decide for them.

Weighing in on the other side of the argument are those who, like George McGovern, a former Democratic candidate for president, are concerned about a general decline of tolerance. In a recent op-ed in the *New York Times*, McGovern eloquently took to task

> those who would deny others the choice to eat meat, wear fur, drink coffee or simply eat extra-large portions of food. . . . While on any day each of us may identify with the restrictive nature of a given campaign, there is a much larger issue here. Where do we draw the line on dictating to each other? How many of these battles can we stand? Whose values should prevail?

It is incumbent upon classical liberals to resist this presumption: that consensual pastimes are a matter for the state to tolerate sometimes but to outlaw when politically expedient. As the 19th-century economist and philosopher John Stuart Mill famously declared, "Over himself, over his own body and mind, the individual is sovereign." To depart from that standard is to put at risk our inheritance, the tradition of individual liberty upon which America was founded. And that would indeed be a reckless gamble.

> "The Internet not only makes highly
> addictive forms of gambling easily
> accessible to everyone, it magnifies the
> potential destructiveness of the addiction."

The Government Should Prohibit Gambling on the Internet

Jon Kyl

Jon Kyl is a Republican senator from Arizona. In 1997, Senator Kyl introduced legislation that would ban all forms of gambling over the Internet. (As of summer 2001, this legislation is still before Congress.) The proposed Internet Gambling Prohibition Act would make it a crime for businesses to offer casino gambling or sports betting services over the Internet. In the following viewpoint, Kyl maintains that the legislation is necessary because of the harm that gambling causes society. He maintains that unrestricted Internet gambling would greatly exacerbate the problem of compulsive gambling and its costs to society.

As you read, consider the following questions:
1. How has Professor John Kindt described Internet gambling, as quoted by Kyl?
2. What 1961 law currently prohibits the use of phone lines for gambling purposes, according to the author?
3. What amateur and professional sports organizations does Kyl say support a ban on Internet gambling?

Excerpted from Jon Kyl's statement before the Senate Judiciary Subcommittee on Technology, Terrorism, and Government Information, March 23, 1999.

From the beginning of time, societies have sought to prohibit most forms of gambling. There are reasons for this
—and they are especially applicable to gambling on the Internet today. Consider the following.

Youth. A recent *New York Times* article warned that "Internet sports betting entices youthful gamblers into potentially costly losses." In the same article, Kevin O'Neill,
deputy director of the Council on Compulsive Gambling
of New Jersey, said that "Internet sports gambling appeals
to college-age people who don't have immediate access to
a neighborhood bookie. . . . It's on the Net and kids think it's
credible, which is scary."

Listen to the testimony of Jeff Pash, the Executive Vice
President of the National Football League, before the Senate Judiciary Committee: "Studies . . . indicate that sports
betting is a growing problem for high school and college
students. . . . As the Internet reaches more and more school
children, Internet gambling is certain to promote even more
gambling among young people."

Families. Gambling often has terrible consequences for
families and communities. According to the Council on
Compulsive Gambling, five percent of all gamblers become
addicted. Many of those turn to crime and commit suicide.
We all pay for those tragedies.

Harm to Businesses and the Economy. Internet gambling is
likely to have a deleterious effect on businesses and the
economy. As Ted Koppel noted in a "Nightline" feature on
Internet gambling, "[l]ast year, 1,333,000 American consumers filed for bankruptcy, thereby eliminating about $40
billion in personal debt. That's of some relevance to all of us
because the $40 billion debt doesn't just disappear. It's redis-
tributed among the rest of us in the form of increased prices
on consumer goods. . . ." He continued: "If anything
promises to increase the level of personal debt in this country, expanding access to gambling should do it."

Professor John Kindt testified before the House Small
Business Committee that a business with 1,000 workers can
anticipate increased personnel costs of $500,000 a year due
to job absenteeism and declining productivity simply by having various forms of legalized gambling accessible.

Addiction. Internet gambling enhances the addictive nature of gambling because it is so easy to do: you don't have to travel; you can just log on to your computer. Professor Kindt has described electronic gambling, like the type being offered in the "virtual casinos" on the Internet, as the "hardcore cocaine of gambling."

An Incredibly Addictive Experience

Gambling online is among the most addictive experiences I've encountered. . . .

Online, you can have your credit card purchase of chips approved more speedily than it would take to walk across a Vegas casino floor to the ATM. You can play far more hands in any hour than you can offline—no waiting for reshuffles, no major waits for slower players. My unofficial estimate: Your action (deals, spins, and so on) moves at three to five times the offline pace. You can avoid boredom by instantly switching from one game to another—again, more quickly than you could in a casino. You can dive into high-stakes games without knowing whether it's Amarillo Slim or a pastor from Dubuque raising you. And there's something about betting from your home, from your den, in your pajamas, that makes it really comfortable to keep on clicking and spinning. At one point in an online blackjack game, I saw my finger clicking on that mouse so quickly, so continually, playing the hands so instantly, that I suddenly had an image of myself as a pigeon in a lab pecking unstoppably for pellets.

Barry Golson, *Yahoo! Internet Life*, March 2001.

As Bernie Horn, the Executive Director of the National Coalition Against Legalized Gaming, testified before the House Judiciary Subcommittee on Crime: "The Internet not only makes highly addictive forms of gambling easily accessible to everyone, it magnifies the potential destructiveness of the addiction. Because of the privacy of an individual and his/her computer terminal, addicts can destroy themselves without anyone ever having the chance to stop them."

Unfair payouts. As Wisconsin Attorney General James Doyle testified before the Senate Judiciary Committee, "[b]ecause [Internet gambling] is unregulated, consumers don't know who is on the other end of the connection. The odds can be easily manipulated and there is no guarantee that fair payouts will occur." "Anyone who gambles over the Internet is making a sucker bet," says William A. Bible, the chair of an Internet gambling subcommittee on the National Gambling Impact Study Commission.

Crime. Further, gambling on the Internet is apt to lead to criminal behavior. Indeed, "Up to 90 percent of pathological gamblers commit crimes to pay off their wagering debts." A University of Illinois study found that for every dollar that states gain from gambling, they pay out three dollars in social and criminal costs.

Cost. According to an article in the March 1999 *ABA Journal*, "Online wagering is generating a $600-million-a-year kitty that some analysts say could reach as high as $100 billion a year by 2006." I want to repeat that: $100 *billion* a year. The article continues: "The number of Web sites offering Internet gambling is growing at a similar rate. In just one year, that number more than quadrupled, going from about 60 in late 1997 to now more than 260 according to some estimates." And a recent HBO in-depth report by Jim Lampley noted that virtual sports books will collect more money from the Super Bowl than all the sports books in Las Vegas combined.

This affects all of us.

A Federal Issue

Not every problem that is national is also necessarily federal. Internet gambling is a *national* problem and a *federal* problem. The Internet is, of course, interstate in nature. States cannot protect their citizens from Internet gambling if *anyone* can transmit it into their states. That is why the State Attorneys General asked for federal legislation to prohibit Internet gambling. In a letter to the Judiciary Committee members, the Chairs of the Association's Internet Working Group stressed the need for *federal* involvement: "[M]ore than any other area of the law, gambling has traditionally been regulated on a state-by-state basis, with little uniformity and minimal federal oversight. The availability of gambling on the Internet, however, threatens to disrupt each state's careful balancing of its own public welfare and fiscal concerns, by making gambling available across state and national boundaries, with little or no regulatory control."

Further, in reaffirming his support for the bill, the former President of NAAG [the National Association of Attorneys General], Wisconsin Attorney General Jim Doyle, wrote: "Internet gambling poses a major challenge for state and local law enforcement officials. I strongly support Senator Kyl's Internet Gambling Prohibition Act. Prohibiting this form of unregulated gambling will protect consumers from fraud and preserve state policies on gambling that have been established by our citizens and our legislators."

The Current Law Is Inadequate

In 1961, Congress passed the Wire Act to prohibit using telephone facilities to receive bets or send gambling information. In addition to penalties imposed upon gambling businesses that violate the law, the Wire Act gives local and state law enforcement authorities the power to direct telecommunication providers to discontinue service to proprietors of gambling services who use the wires to conduct illegal gambling activity. But, as pointed out in the March 1999 *ABA Journal*, "The problem with current federal law is that the communications technology it specifies is dated and limited." The advent of the Internet, a communications medium not envisioned by the Wire Act, requires enactment of a new law to address activities in cyberspace not contemplated by the drafters of the older law.

The Internet Gambling Prohibition Act ensures that the law keeps pace with technology. The bill bans gambling on the Internet, just as the Wire Act prohibited gambling over the wires. And it does not limit the subject of gambling to sports. The bill is similar to the one that the Senate, by an overwhelming 90-10 vote, attached to the Commerce-Justice-State Appropriations bill in 1998. Let me take a moment to explain the bill.

The bill covers sports gambling *and* casino games. Businesses that offer gambling over the Internet can be fined in an amount equal to the amount that the business received in bets via the Internet or $20,000, whichever is greater, and/or imprisoned for not more than four years. To address concerns raised by the Department of Justice, the bill (like the Wire Act) does not contain penalties for individual bettors.

Such betting will, of course, still be the subject of state law.

The bill contains a strong enforcement mechanism. At the request of the United States or a State, a district court may enter a temporary restraining order or an injunction against any person to prevent a violation of the bill, following due notice and based on a finding of substantial probability that there has been a violation of the law. In effect, the illegal website will have its service cut off. I have worked with the Internet service providers to address concerns they raised about how they would cut off service. . . .

In sum, the Internet Gambling Prohibition Act brings federal law up to date. With the advent of new, sophisticated technology, the Wire Act is becoming outdated. The Internet Gambling Prohibition Act corrects that problem.

Widespread, Bipartisan Support

I would like to take a moment to review the consideration of the bill during the last Congress. In July 1997, the Judiciary Subcommittee on Technology held a hearing on S. 474 [Senate resolution 474 is the bill that would make the Internet Gambling Prohibition Act into law]. A wide variety of people testified in support of the legislation: Senator Richard Bryan; Wisconsin Attorney General Jim Doyle, the then-President of the National Association of Attorneys General; Jeff Pash, Counsel to the National Football League; Ann Geer, Chair of the National Coalition Against Gambling Expansion; and Anthony Cabot, professor at the International Gaming Institute.

Ann Geer stated that "Internet gambling would multiply addiction exponentially, increasing access and magnifying the potential destructiveness of the addiction. Addicts would literally click their mouse and bet the house."

As I noted earlier, Wisconsin Attorney General James Doyle testified that "gambling on the Internet is a very dumb bet. Because it is unregulated . . . odds can be easily manipulated and there is no guarantee that fair payouts will occur. . . . Internet gambling threatens to disrupt the system. It crosses state and national borders with little or no regulatory control. Federal authorities must take the lead in this area."

Additionally, in June 1999, the Judiciary Committee held

a hearing on FBI oversight at which I said to [former] FBI Director Louis Freeh: "the testimony from other Department of Justice and FBI witnesses has supported our legislation to conform the crime of gambling on the Internet to existing law. And I would just like a reconfirmation of the FBI's support for that legislation." Director Freeh replied "yes, I think it's a very effective change. We certainly support it."

The Judiciary Subcommittee on Technology passed S. 474 unanimously; the full Judiciary Committee passed S. 474 by voice vote.

In July 1998, by a 90 to 10 vote, the Internet Gambling Prohibition Act was attached to the Commerce-Justice-State Appropriations bill. In the House, the bill passed Representative McCollum's Crime Subcommittee unanimously, but due to the lateness of the session, the bill failed to move farther in the House and was not included in the final CJS bill.

The bill has broad bipartisan support in Congress and the strong support of law enforcement. As I just mentioned, FBI Director Freeh has testified that the bill makes a "very effective change" to the law and the National Association of Attorneys General sent a letter supporting S. 474 to all Senators. . . .

Florida Attorney General Bob Butterworth also wrote a letter stressing the support of the states for this bill: "The adoption of a resolution on this issue by NAAG represents overwhelming support from the states for a bill which, in essence, increases the federal presence in an area of primary state concern. However, it is clear that the federal government has an important role in this issue which crosses state as well as international boundaries."

In the 105th Congress, S. 474 was strongly supported by professional and amateur sports. The National Football League, the National Collegiate Athletic Association, the National Hockey League, the National Basketball Association, Major League Soccer, and Major League Baseball sent a joint letter of support to all Senators.

I would like to read a passage from this letter:

Despite existing federal and state laws prohibiting gambling on professional and college sports, sports gambling over the Internet has become a serious—and growing—national problem. Many Internet gambling operations originate from offshore locations outside the U.S. The number of offshore Internet gambling websites has grown from two in 1996 to over 70 today. It is estimated that Internet sites will book over $600 million in sports bets in 1998, up from $60 million just two years ago. These websites not only permit offshore gambling operations to solicit and take bets from the United States in defiance of federal and state law but also enable gamblers and would-be gamblers in the U.S. to place illegal sports wagers over the Internet from the privacy of their own home or office.

The letter concludes: "We strongly urge you to vote in favor of S. 474 when it is considered on the Senate floor."

On behalf of the NCAA, Bill Saum testified in February 1999 before the National Gambling Impact Study Commission on the dangers of Internet gambling:

> "Internet gambling provides college students with the opportunity to place wagers on professional and college sporting events from the privacy of his or her campus residence. Internet gambling offers the student virtual anonymity. With nothing more than a credit card, the possibility exists for any student-athlete to place a wager via the Internet and then attempt to influence the outcome of the contest while participating on the court or the playing field. There is no question the advent of Internet sports gambling poses a direct threat to all sports organizations that, first and foremost, must ensure the integrity of each contest played."

An Effective Deterrent

The Internet offers fantastic opportunities. Unfortunately, some would exploit those opportunities to commit crimes and take advantage of others. Indeed, as Professor Kindt stated on "Nightline," "Once you go to Internet gambling, you've maximized the speed, you've maximized the acceptability and the accessibility. It's going to be in-your-face gambling, which is going to have severe detrimental effects to society. . . . It's the crack cocaine of creating new pathological gamblers."

Internet gambling is a serious problem. Society has always prohibited most forms of gambling because it can have a devastating effect on people and families, and it often leads to crime and other corruption. The Internet Gambling Prohibition Act will curb the spread of online gambling.

*"The very architecture of the Internet
renders gambling prohibition futile."*

The Government Should Not Prohibit Gambling on the Internet

Tom W. Bell

Tom W. Bell is an assistant professor at Chapman University
Law School and an adjunct scholar at the Cato Institute, a
free-market think tank in Washington, D.C. The following
viewpoint is adapted from testimony that Bell gave before
the National Gambling Impact Study Commission, a federal
panel charged with assessing the effects of legalized gambling. In it, Bell asserts that the spread of Internet gambling
is inevitable. Even if the U.S. government bans Internet
gambling, he points out, gamblers will be able to access
gambling websites based in other countries. Fortunately,
Bell concludes, Internet gambling is not as dangerous as opponents have claimed.

As you read, consider the following questions:
1. What three benefits does Bell claim Internet gambling
   offers?
2. What analogy does the author use to illustrate why a
   prohibition on Internet gambling will not work?
3. How much money did the Internet gambling industry
   generate in 1997, according to Bell, and how much of it
   was from the United States?

Excerpted from Tom W. Bell's testimony before the National Gambling Impact
Study Commission, May 21, 1998.

Thank you for inviting me to testify today on the relative merits of prohibiting Internet gambling versus legalizing it. The issue certainly deserves our careful consideration—but not because public debate will determine whether Internet gambling gets prohibited or legalized. No amount of debate will do that. Ultimately, it does not even matter whether legislators and law enforcement officials try to outlaw Internet gambling. Public deliberation and government action will determine whether legalized Internet gambling comes slowly and painfully or quickly and cleanly—hardly a trivial matter. All facts indicate, however, that sooner or later Americans will legally gamble over the Internet.

My testimony today will describe some of the factors that will frustrate attempts to prohibit Internet gambling and compel its eventual legalization. I will focus on three factors:

First, Internet technology renders prohibition futile. The Internet's inherently open architecture already hobbles law enforcement officials, while relentless technological innovation ensures that they will only fall farther and farther behind.

Second, as an international network, the Internet offers an instant detour around merely domestic prohibitions. Principles of national sovereignty will prevent the U.S. from forcing other countries to enforce a ban on Internet gambling, and it takes only one safe harbor abroad to ensure that U.S. citizens can gamble over the Internet.

Third, consumer demand for Internet gambling and the states' demand for tax revenue will create enormous political pressure for legalization. The law enforcement community, which has until recently enjoyed the media spotlight, will quickly find its calls for prohibition drowned out by these and other political forces.

Since the hard, cold facts about the inevitable failure of prohibition will undoubtedly depress some decent and well-intentioned people, I will leaven my analysis with some comforting words about Internet gambling. A dispassionate account reveals that Internet gambling offers several benefits:

- Internet gambling will drive network development;
- It will provide a more wholesome environment than real-world casinos; and

- It will benefit consumers by increasing competition in gambling services.

Before launching into the details of why legalization will trump the prohibition of Internet gambling, and why that outcome should cause no great alarm, allow me to clear away a preliminary objection. Some proponents of a ban on Internet gambling argue that if prohibition will not work then neither will any scheme of regulation. Such an argument fundamentally misunderstands a basic principle of governance, however: Regulations can succeed even where prohibition fails if they offer benefits that exceed their burdens. That is why people do not illegally shoot craps in Las Vegas alleys. In the case of Internet gambling, the benefits of winning an official stamp of approval might convince an online casino to submit to regulation, even if that same casino could easily flout a total ban on its business. Exactly how much regulation will the Internet gambling industry tolerate? In all likelihood, not very much—but only practical experience can settle that question.

Internet Technology Renders Prohibition Futile

The very architecture of the Internet renders gambling prohibition futile. In contrast to telephone communications, which typically travel over circuit switched networks, Internet communications use packet switching. Each Internet message gets broken into discrete packets, which travel over various and unpredictable routes until received and reassembled at the message's destination. In other words, sending a message over the Internet is a bit like corresponding with someone by writing a letter, chopping it up, and mailing each piece separately to the same address. The recipient can piece it together but anyone snooping on your correspondence has a tougher go of it.

Understanding Internet communications as akin to the postal system clarifies why gambling prohibition just will not work. Imagine telling the postal service that it must henceforth crack down on all letters conveying information used in illegal gambling. It would rightly object that it already has its hands full just delivering the mail and that it lacks the equipment and personnel to snoop through every letter. It would furthermore note that it could not always tell which messages relate to illegal activities. People use "bet" and "wager" in everyday conversations whereas gamblers often speak in code. Meanwhile, customers of the mail service will strongly object to having the postal service paw through their correspondence.

© Mike Shelton. Reprinted with special permission of King Features Syndicate.

Nor can prohibitionists expect the postal service to simply stop delivering mail to and from certain addresses associated with illegal gambling. The postal service will again object to the burdens of implementing such a program. Citizens will again object to law enforcement officials spying on private correspondence. More importantly, though, trying to cut off certain addresses will simply fail to stop gambling. Gamblers will rely on P.O. boxes, which they can change at a moment's notice, and simply drop off outgoing correspondence with no return address.

All these considerations apply with equal or greater force to Internet gambling. Compared to the postal system, the Internet makes it easier to encrypt messages, to change addresses, and to send and receive messages anonymously. Internet service providers would thus find it impossible to discriminate between illicit gaming information and other Internet traffic. Furthermore, in contrast to the quasi-public and monolithic postal system, the Internet relies on thousands of separate and wholly private service providers to carry out its deliveries. All of them would stridently object to the burdens of enforcing a ban on Internet traffic. More than a few would simply refuse to cooperate.

Does that sound like a pessimistic account? To the contrary, it merely describes the current situation. As technological innovation continues to drive the development of Internet communications, law enforcement officials will fall farther and farther behind illegal gamblers.

Given these technological constraints, prohibiting Internet gambling plainly will not work as intended. As an unintended side effect, however, prohibition would sorely compromise the cost, efficiency, and security of Internet communications. Given the inevitable failure of technical fixes, legalizing Internet gambling offers the only viable solution.

Internet Gambling Can Escape Domestic Prohibitions

Outlawing Internet gaming services domestically will simply push the business overseas. Federal law enforcement agents admit that they cannot stop overseas gaming operations. "International Internet gambling? We can't do anything about it," Department of Justice spokesman John Russell said, "That's the bottom line." Even Sen. Jon Kyl has confessed that "this would be a very difficult kind of activity to regulate because we don't have jurisdiction over the people abroad who are doing it."

Both practical and legal barriers prevent any domestic ban on Internet gambling from having international effect. Because the Internet provides instant access to overseas sites, any domestic prohibition on the offer of gaming services will have to cover the whole planet to work. American law enforcement agents can—and recently did—arrest local citizens accused of running Internet gambling businesses, but smart operators will quickly learn to set up abroad and stay there.

Gaming services can find ample shelter overseas. A growing number of countries, including Australia, New Zealand, Antigua, and Costa Rica, have decided to legalize and license Internet gaming services. Principles of international law, which protect each country's sovereignty, bar the United States from extraditing its citizens merely for violating domestic anti-gambling laws. Furthermore, the Sixth Amendment of the Constitution's Bill of Rights prohibits the criminal prosecution of those who remain overseas while operating Internet gambling sites. Law enforcement officials in the United States can thus neither arrest nor sentence anyone who offers Internet gambling services from a safe harbor abroad.

The Powerful Demand for Internet Gambling

Americans love to gamble. Having already embraced traditional games of chance, they will almost certainly extend a warm welcome to Internet gambling. At least 56% of Americans gambled in 1995. Few Americans regard it as immoral; a 1993 survey found that only 25% of non-gamblers cited moral or religious reasons. By current estimates, Americans will wager more than $600 billion in 1998—nearly $2,400 for every man, woman, and child. About $100 billion of that sum will go toward illegal bets, demonstrating that Americans already pay little heed to anti-gambling laws.

Regardless of its legality, Americans have already shown that they support the nascent Internet gambling industry. Analysts calculate that of the $1 billion in revenues that Internet gambling generated in 1997, about $600 million came from the United States. Online casinos will have worldwide revenues of some $7.9 billion by the year 2001, $3.5 billion of it coming from U.S. consumers. Because the Internet offers bettors instant access to overseas gambling sites and relative safety from prosecution, online gambling will grow regardless of what prohibitionists want.

Soon, though, the prohibitionists will have more than consumer demand to worry about. Law enforcement agents have seized the media spotlight by telling scary stories and demanding new powers to crush Internet gambling. As the futility of prohibition becomes more and more evident, however, cooler heads in state revenue departments will begin to see Internet gambling as a huge new cash cow. Prohibition merely assures that Internet gamblers will ship their money to places like Antigua, New Zealand, and Australia. State governors and legislatures will soon demand a share of that bounty. The same political forces that have led to the widespread legalization of lottery, casino, and riverboat gambling will thus eventually lead to the legalization of Internet gambling.

Indeed, this trend towards the legalization of Internet gambling has already started. Initially, Senator Kyl's Internet Gambling Prohibition Act of 1997 banned every sort of online commercial contest, everywhere in the United States, for everyone involved. Facing a storm of objections, he recently drafted an amendment to the bill that would allow a variety of types of online gambling, such as interstate off-track bet pooling and intrastate parimutuel and lottery bets. Representative Bob Goodlatte once defended his own bill to prohibit Internet gambling with the claim that existing laws "have been turned on their head" by the Internet because "[n]o longer do people have to leave the comfort of their homes" to access casinos. In fact, however, nine states already allow their citizens to access professional gaming services at home via telecommunications devices. Legalized Internet gambling, far from revolutionizing American culture, will come as a natural extension of current social and technological trends.

The Benefits of Internet Gambling

I have set forth a number of reasons why attempts to prohibit Internet gambling will inevitably fail and give way to legalization. Mere futility hardly suffices to bar bad public policy, however. Allow me, then, to adduce some reasons why we should welcome the legalization of Internet gambling.

Internet gambling will encourage the private sector to develop network capacity and commerce. Just as real-world casinos have competed to build the most innovative and appealing environments, so too will Internet gaming services compete to offer the flashiest graphics and most sophisticated user interfaces. That competition will, as a nice side-benefit, result in broader bandwidth and better software for all sorts of Internet applications.

Critics of real-world casinos fault them for luring consumers into windowless caverns far from the real world, with gambling traps at every turn and free-flowing booze. Regardless of the validity of such criticisms, they certainly do not apply to Internet gambling. To the contrary, consumers who log on from home computers will find it impossible to escape phone calls, barking dogs, and all the other distractions of the real world. Internet gambling thus offers a more wholesome environment than its real-world counterpart.

Lastly, we should never forget that gamblers deserve all the benefits that other consumers of entertainment services enjoy—including the benefits of competition. By giving consumers cheap and easy access to a variety of gaming opportunities, the Internet will bring competition to an industry that has long enjoyed the shelter of highly restrictive licensing practices. Gamblers will no longer have to fly to Las Vegas to play the slots, drive to the nearest authorized track to play the horses, or even walk to the corner store to play the state lotto. Consumers can already play these and other games at home via the many Internet web sites—over 50 and growing—that offer gambling services. Prohibiting Internet gambling will not make it inaccessible, whereas legalizing it will put the benefits of increased competition within the rule of law.

> "*Sports wagering threatens the integrity of sports, it puts student-athletes in a vulnerable position, [and] it can serve as a gateway behavior for adolescent gamblers.*"

The Government Should Ban Betting on College Sports

James C. Dobson

James C. Dobson is founder and president of Focus on the Family, a Christian ministry based in Colorado Springs, Colorado. In the following viewpoint, he argues that the federal government should prohibit wagering on college sports. According to Dobson sports betting is common among college students and has corrupted many student-athletes. Sports bettors usually don't bet on whether a team will simply win or lose, but also on whether the team will win by a certain number of points. In some cases, athletes have been paid to "shave points," or purposely try not to score as much as they normally would, in order to rig games. In Dobson's view, a total ban on college sports betting is necessary to avoid these scandals.

As you read, consider the following questions:

1. How much do Nevada casinos make off of betting on college football and basketball games, according to Dobson?
2. In the survey cited by Dobson, what percentage of male football and basketball players admitted to betting on sports?
3. What percentage of male college students bet on sports, according to the author?

From "Gambling with the Future of College Sports," by James C. Dobson, *USA Today*, May 2001. Copyright © 2001 by the Society for the Advancement of Education. Reprinted with permission.

Nothing beats an October Saturday afternoon at the Los Angeles County Coliseum watching my beloved University of Southern California football team taking it to the likes of the University of Notre Dame or UCLA. Even though Trojan victories have been somewhat scarce of late, I still try mightily to arrange my schedule each fall to be in the Coliseum's sun-soaked stands for at least one game.

Tens of millions of other Americans share my passion for college football. We marvel at the talent, teamwork, determination, and strategy poured into those three- or four-hour battles, and we walk away, win or lose, entertained by the experience. Yet, this treasured pastime is imperiled. A toxic threat looms over the entire collegiate athletic landscape. That threat is gambling.

Point-Shaving and Game-Fixing

For two years, I served on the National Gambling Impact Study Commission. In June, 1999, my eight colleagues and I authored a final report replete with more than 70 recommendations to Congress and state and tribal governments. It was during the commission's proceedings that I awakened to the tremendous dangers posed by gambling on collegiate sports. In our final report, we concluded: "Sports wagering threatens the integrity of sports, it puts student-athletes in a vulnerable position, it can serve as a gateway behavior for adolescent gamblers, and it can devastate individuals and careers."

That is why I authored a recommendation, subsequently approved by the commission, to ban gambling on collegiate and amateur athletic events. That recommendation became the basis for Congressional legislation, spearheaded by Senators John McCain (R.-Ariz.) and Sam Brownback (R.-Kan.) and Representatives Tim Roemer (D.-Ind.) and Lindsey Graham (R.-S.C.).

This long-overdue legislation would close the "Nevada loophole" left open by the Professional and Amateur Sports Protection Act, passed by Congress in 1992. That bill made it illegal in 49 states to gamble on college sporting events, with the glaring exception of Nevada. As a result, Nevada casinos now reap close to $1,000,000,000 a year in wagers on college football and basketball games.

This bonanza for Nevada wagering establishments comes at a tremendous price to our colleges and universities—and to the athletes themselves. According to National Collegiate Athletic Association president Cedric Dempsey, "The millions of dollars wagered legally on college sports has resulted in more 'point-shaving' and 'game-fixing' scandals in the 1990s than the previous five decades combined." Those scandals have ensnared dozens of athletes from some of the nation's most prestigious academic institutions:

- At Northwestern University, 11 student-athletes were convicted in gambling scandals involving the school's athletic teams. Among them were the football team's star tailback, Dennis Lundy, who admitted to intentionally fumbling the ball at the goal line in a 1994 game against the University of Iowa so he could win a bet. Two Northwestern basketball players were convicted of trying to fix three games in exchange for bribes from gamblers.
- Thirteen members of the Boston College football team were suspended for gambling in 1996, including two who bet against the Eagles.
- The all-time leading passer at the University of Maryland, Scott Milanovich, was suspended for four games in 1995 for betting on college sports.
- Arizona State All-America point guard Stevin ("Hedake") Smith sacrificed a promising pro basketball career and ended up in prison after he and a teammate were found guilty of shaving points during the 1993–94 season.

Gambling Among Athletes and Sports Officials

Surveys indicate that gambling is indeed rampant among male college athletes. In 1999, researchers at the University of Michigan surveyed 460 NCAA Division I male football and basketball players. More than 45% admitted to betting on sports, despite NCAA regulations prohibiting such activity. Even more disconcerting, 5 percent admitted to succumbing to gambling pressures, either by providing inside information to gamblers, betting on a game they participated in, or accepting money for performing poorly. If these results can be generalized—and they very well may understate the problem—approximately four or five players on every Division I college football team and one player on the majority of collegiate basketball teams are being influenced by gambling.

These findings mirror a 1996 study of 650 collegiate football and basketball players conducted by the University of Cincinnati. In that survey, 4 percent of respondents admitted gambling on games in which they played, while 0.5% confessed to receiving money from a gambler for not playing well.

The Insidiousness of Point-Shaving

The most insidious aspect of legalized betting on college teams is the point spread. It raises dark questions where there should be none. For someone betting the spread, it matters not whether your favorite team wins, but rather by how much they win or lose. Las Vegas casinos set a point spread for each game. It's published in newspapers across the U.S. and used by illegal bookmakers. . . .

Here's how the betting lines work: say a casino's sports book favors the Duke basketball team to beat Florida State by 11 points. If you bet on Duke, but Duke wins by only 8 points, you lose. If you bet on Florida State, you win.

And that's the source of a nagging question—not just for gamblers but for fans, coaches and university administrators. If a team beats its opponents but not by the official Vegas spread, were the games fixed? Did players deliberately miss shots? Did they intentionally foul? Did they purposely fail to block shots?

Therein lies the sinister beauty of rigging a game by shaving points: It's nearly impossible to detect.

Donald L. Barlett et al., *Time*, September 25, 2000.

Players are not the only ones susceptible to gambling pressures. In March, 2000, the University of Michigan released a survey of 640 college sports officials. Forty percent admitted to betting on sports. Twelve said they knew of other officials who had not called a game fairly for gambling reasons.

The rightfully heightened concern about gambling on collegiate sports has cast suspicion on all who are involved. Former Indiana University basketball coach Bob Knight fueled the fire in 1999 when, in an ESPN interview, he said, "If we only knew the truth about games that were controlled by officials having gambling interests, I think it would be amazing." Media-circulated rumors of gambling scandals surrounding UCLA's 1999 Rose Bowl squad and Louisiana State University's 1998 football team turned out to be groundless.

Broad Support of a Ban

Clearly, a problem exists. That is why the pending legislation in Congress [which failed to pass in 2001] has the strong support of the National Collegiate Athletic Association, university presidents, and athletic directors. A veritable "who's who" of college coaches signed a letter to Congress urging passage of the bill. Among the more than 60 signatories were basketball coaches Mike Krzyzewski (Duke University), Tubby Smith (University of Kentucky), and Roy Williams (University of Kansas), as well as football coaches Bobby Bowden (Florida State University), Joe Paterno (Pennsylvania State University), and Frank Solich (University of Nebraska).

University of South Carolina football coach Lou Holtz, formerly the head coach at Notre Dame, also signed the letter. In 2000, he appeared on my daily radio broadcast to plead for passage of the bill. On that broadcast, Holtz described how one of his former placekickers, shortly after finishing his career at Notre Dame, destroyed his reputation and wound up in prison after becoming embroiled in the Northwestern gambling scandal. Holtz also described how his teams are sometimes booed by the home fans—even after a victory— simply because they do not cover the point spread.

The vast majority of Congress, Democrats and Republicans, supports this legislation. Even college gambling proponents concede that these bills would pass overwhelmingly in both houses. The two companion bills passed by wide margins in the Senate Commerce Committee and the House Judiciary Committee, but that is as far as they have gone.

What is the hold-up? It is the gambling industry. Casinos poured millions into the campaign coffers of both parties during the 2000 elections. Further, the American Gaming Association has shelled out millions more in a full court press lobbying effort. It has bought such fire with Congress that House and Senate leaders refuse to even allow a vote. In fact, not a single leader in either house—Republican or Democrat—would even grant a meeting with the NCAA, despite repeated requests, all the while maintaining an open-door policy with the gift-bearing gambling industry.

Casino Industry Excuses

During the Congressional debate over the legislation, casino operators have thrown out a bevy of desperate excuses to defend their indefensible, but lucrative, enterprise. From one side of their mouths, they claim that this legislation would be, in the words of Sen. Richard Bryan (D.-Nev.), "an illegal bookie's dream," by driving Nevada's business underground. Out of the other, they contend that the amount gambled legally on sports betting is an inconsequential one percent, compared to the total that is bet illegally. The truth is, no one has the slightest idea how much is gambled illegally on college sports, although all agree that it is a substantial sum.

Far from the sharp distinctions that gambling apologists attempt to draw between illegal sports gambling and that which takes place in Nevada, the reality is that legal and illegal forms enjoy a symbiotic relationship. Our commission's final report states succinctly: "Legal sports wagering—especially the publication in the media of Las Vegas and offshore generated point spreads—fuels a much larger amount of illegal sports wagering."

During our deliberations, it became clear that the apparent legitimacy given to sports gambling by Nevada's casinos has confused the public. Many, if not most, Americans do not understand that it is illegal everywhere else. Nowhere is this more evident than on college campuses. A study released in 2000 revealed that 39% of male college students gamble on sports. One of the Boston College football players involved in that school's gambling scandal said, "To tell the truth, it never crossed my mind it was illegal, it was so commonplace." In his testimony before the House Judiciary Committee, Holtz stated, "People in general, college students in particular, have the belief that betting on college athletics is okay because it is legal in Nevada."

The relationship between the two forms of sports gambling is even more direct. Kevin Pendergast, the former Notre Dame placekicker, placed a $20,000 bet in Las Vegas because local bookies could not accept such a large bet. "Without the option of betting money in Nevada," Pendergast told members of Congress, "the Northwestern basketball point-shaving scandal would not have occurred"

Four gamblers in the Arizona State basketball case placed a total of 61 bets at Las Vegas wagering establishments, totaling hundreds of thousands of dollars. In 2000, Chicago authorities broke up a multi million-dollar sports betting ring. The operators, some of whom have been convicted of mob-related crimes, used cell phones to relay bets to Las Vegas on pro and college football and basketball games, according to a U.S. Attorney.

Casino moguls also trot out the state's rights argument, all the while struggling to maintain a straight face. The argument is ludicrous. Nevada, fully cognizant of the dangers inherent in sports gambling, until recently prohibited betting on teams within the state.

The casinos' tactics include trying to shift the blame and criticize the NCAA for not doing enough to stop illegal gambling. In recent years, though, the NCAA has launched an aggressive, multi-front attack aimed at curtailing gambling and its influence on college sports.

Three NCAA staffers are assigned to a gambling task force. In April, 2000, the association's management council established automatic penalties for gambling involvement among players, including a complete loss of eligibility for participants who bet on their own games. Representatives from the FBI are brought in each year to address Division I athletes on the dangers of gambling. The NCAA airs public-service announcements, featuring prominent student-athletes, during high-profile televised sporting events. The organization also has instituted random background checks on officials who work the NCAA Division I basketball tournament each March. In addition, the NCAA continues to sponsor research, distribute relevant resources to schools and athletes, and is currently working to develop a curriculum for all college students regarding gambling's dangers.

These efforts are destined for minimal success, however,

unless all 50 states present a united front against gambling on college sports. As long as the status quo exists, the only question is "when," not "if," the next college gambling scandal will erupt. The temptation is simply too great. Smith, the former Arizona State basketball player, wrote in *Sports Illustrated*, "I can tell you how easily players can be drawn into fixing games. Poor, naive teenagers plus rich, greedy gamblers equals disaster."

We should not have to wonder if our team's game is already fixed so that a handful of casino moguls can fatten their bottom lines. Let us protect college athletics from any more disasters. Ban gambling on college sports.

> *"There is no persuasive evidence that legal sports betting in Nevada is responsible for the betting scandals and illegal gambling everywhere else."*

The Government Should Not Ban Betting on College Sports

Danny Sheridan

Danny Sheridan is a sports analyst for *USA Today* and the author of several books on sports betting. The following viewpoint is adapted from testimony Sheridan gave in April 2001 before a Senate committee that was considering legislation that would have banned betting on college sports. Such betting is already illegal in every state except Nevada, notes Sheridan, but illegal sports betting nevertheless occurs throughout the country. Therefore, Sheridan reasons, banning sports betting in Nevada would not reduce the illegal betting that occurs outside of Nevada. Instead, he argues, such a ban would have a harmful effect: The Nevada Gaming Commission, which investigates incidents of game-fixing and other corruption, would no longer monitor sports betting.

As you read, consider the following questions:
1. How much money did the National Gambling Impact Study Commission estimate that Americans wager annually on sports, according to the author?
2. What fraction of the money that is gambled legally in Nevada is bet on college sports, according to Sheridan?
3. What message would the Amateur Sports Integrity Act send to young people, in the author's view?

Excerpted from Danny Sheridan's testimony before the Senate Commerce Committee, April 26, 2001.

My name is Danny Sheridan, and I have been involved with sports and the sports promotion business for more than 25 years. I have published college and pro football magazines, written about sports in a variety of national publications, and have been the host of a number of sports TV and radio shows. I am a lifelong resident of Mobile, Alabama, and a graduate of the University of Alabama School of Business.

I have written exclusively for *USA Today* since its inception in 1982. For *USA Today*, I set the daily odds on every sport along with political and esoteric odds—for example, will Alan Greenspan lower the interest rate, and if so, by how much. My sports and political predictions have been featured on every major network and nearly every major newspaper and radio station in the country. I plan to continue setting these odds and providing them to *USA Today* even if this legislation [the Amateur Sports Integrity Act] is passed.

However, I'm not just a sports—and sometimes political—analyst. I am friends with many high profile college and NFL coaches as well as many NFL and NBA owners. I have spoken at or visited most of the colleges and universities in the United States, and have talked to thousands of students about their concerns about sports betting on their campuses. I've also interviewed many of the world's biggest legal, illegal, and offshore bookmakers.

I'm sure there are a lot of people brighter than me at this hearing; however, I'm confident in saying that my predictions, contacts and knowledge of the sports world would stack up against anyone in this room.

That's why I'm here today.

I do not bet on sports, don't smoke or drink alcohol, but I do recognize, like you, that in a free society people do these things, sometimes to excess.

I commend you for having the courage to take on the tough issue of fighting illegal gambling. However, I want to warn you of the serious, unintended, and adverse consequences that will surely result from the passage and implementation of this legislation. Your attempt to eliminate legal college sports wagering—while well intentioned—would only result in an increase in illegal college sports gambling and an increase in the amount of fixing and point shaving schemes and scandals.

Currently, approximately 99 percent of all sports gambling takes place illegally outside of Nevada. In 1999, the National Gaming Impact Study Commission estimated that illegal sports wagering was as much as $380 billion—but I think that it's higher. An estimated 40 million Americans currently wager $6 billion illegally every weekend during the entire 20-week college and pro football season alone.

A Ban on College Sports Betting Will Not Help Young People

I would like to make 3 brief, specific, and interrelated points that are relevant to the committee's deliberations on the *Amateur Sports Integrity Act*:

- Prohibiting legalized sports gambling likely will have little impact on young people; gambling already is illegal and unsanctioned for student athletes;

- Prohibiting sports gambling for the vast majority who do it safely and legally risks making matters worse by creating an "underground" market;

- Passing legislation that likely is unenforceable inadvertently diminishes respect for the rule of law. . . .

America likes to gamble, and since the early days of civilization, people have shown a penchant to gamble on sports. We should not lose sight of the fact that the vast majority of Americans regulate their impulses without difficulty and are "healthy" gamblers. These circumstances make our efforts to protect young people much more complicated than simply prohibiting sports gambling in Nevada.

Howard J. Shaffer, testimony before the Senate Commerce Committee, April 26, 2001.

Comparatively, legal and regulated sports wagering in Nevada is only 1 percent—a tiny fraction—of all of the betting that occurs on sports in this country. And of the approximately $2.3 billion that is legally wagered in Nevada, only about one-third—an even smaller percentage—is bet on college sports.

These figures just show that there is no persuasive evidence that legal sports betting in Nevada is responsible for the betting scandals and illegal gambling everywhere else.

Nevada's legal sports books serve as a legal watchdog for college sports. The point shaving scandals 5 years ago surfaced only because there is a legal authority that exists to watch over the game and betting activity. So in essence, the proposed legislation would remove the only viable enforcement mechanism to monitor and report the fixing of college sports games.

If you take college sports wagering out of Nevada, 100 percent of all NCAA betting would go on illegally. The Nevada Gaming Commission has an incentive to report the fixing of games and to continue to police sports betting to ensure that it's clean. It is legally required to monitor and report suspicious activity, and has done an excellent job monitoring college sports betting. But if you get rid of legal college sports wagering, a person who wants to fix a game will no longer have to worry about the Nevada Gaming Commission, but only about the bookie he placed the bet with and the players involved.

The proposed legislation would make it impossible to monitor and report the fixing of games. The effect of this legislation would be like removing the Securities and Exchange Commission (SEC) from monitoring and policing the stock market. Does the SEC prevent all insider trading? Of course not, but it lets would be criminals know that they'll be prosecuted. In Nevada, you can't bet on a college game through a dummy corporation—you have to do so in person and be 21 or over—and most people know if you fix a sporting event, you'll eventually get caught and prosecuted.

The NCAA and its supporters also argue that legal betting in Nevada sends a mixed message about gambling to young people. But I'm not sure what mixed message they are talking about.

Gambling and betting is a widely accepted form of recreation in this country and has been an integral part of our history. When our founding fathers needed money to finance the American Revolution, they held a lottery. Today, 47 states permit lotteries, horse and dog racing, commercial and Indian casinos, and/or video poker. Only Hawaii, Utah, and Tennessee have no form of legalized gambling. Since our culture sends the message that gambling is mainstream recreation, it will only make matters worse to deal with illegal sports gambling by making it illegal in Nevada, the one state where these activities are legal and closely monitored. Finally, it's simply not reasonable to assume that the impulse to gamble can be controlled or reduced by legislation, particularly in this age of Internet gambling, which allows anyone to bet through an offshore sports betting site or casino or both just by the flick of a key on their computer.

So yes, the passage of this legislation would send a clear message to this country's young people. That message is: We want to cut down on sports gambling and game-fixing so let's ignore the real problem and the impact this legislation would have on college sports. Now that is a scary mixed message.

Again, I believe that the NCAA and its supporters are well intentioned and are only trying to do the best to protect students and college sports. But the idea that Nevada is to blame for the spread of illegal gambling in this country is preposterous. If the NCAA and its proponents think that the passage of this legislation would have any effect on illegal college sports wagering—by young people or adults—they are completely wrong.

Finally, *opposing* this legislation goes *against* my financial interests. If it were to pass, it would benefit me financially. I also have no financial interest in any casinos or Nevada-dependent companies. With this in mind, I hope that this also shows you that my testimony is unbiased and honest.

So I leave you with these odds and a prediction: pass this legislation and I am 100 percent certain that there will be an increase in game fixing and other point shaving schemes and major college sports scandals—exactly the opposite from what I know you are trying to accomplish.

Periodical Bibliography

The following articles have been selected to supplement the diverse views presented in this chapter. Addresses are provided for periodicals not indexed in the *Readers' Guide to Periodical Literature*, the *Alternative Press Index*, the *Social Sciences Index*, or the *Index to Legal Periodicals and Books*.

Donald L. Barlett et al.	"Throwing the Game," *Time*, September 25, 2000.
Tom W. Bell	"Gambler's Web," *Reason*, October 1999.
Christian Science Monitor	"A Gambling E-Nation?" July 21, 2000.
Warren Cohen	"Don't Bet on Gambling Reform Anytime Soon," *U.S. News & World Report*, June 14, 1999.
Economist	"Betting Against the House," September 4, 1999.
Gerald Eugene Forshey	"Lonely Crusade: Fighting the Gambling Industry," *Christian Century*, November 11, 1998.
James Ledbetter	"Shades of Gray," *Reason*, October 1999.
Marci McDonald	"Betting the House," *U.S. News & World Report*, October 16, 2000.
Richard McGowan	"The Rise of Casino Gaming," *World & I*, March 1997.
Dan McGraw	"The National Bet," *U.S. News & World Report*, April 7, 1997.
National Review	"Know When to Fold 'Em," July 12, 1999.
New Republic	"Gaming the System," July 12, 1999.
Matt Richtel	"The Casino on the Desktop," *New York Times*, March 29, 2001.
William S. Saum	"Sports Gambling in College: Cracking Down on Illegal Betting," *USA Today*, July 1999.
Jacob Sullum	"Some Bets Are Off," *Reason*, June 9, 1999.

For Further Discussion

Chapter 1

1. In your opinion, is gambling immoral in any way, and, if so, how? Discuss the Alberta Conference of Catholic Bishops' arguments in your answer.

2. Frank J. Fahrenkopf Jr., president of the American Gaming Association, writes that "we . . . will continue to defend the rights of our customers." What rights do you think he is referring to? Do you feel that individuals have a right to gamble? Why or why not?

3. Based on the viewpoints by Michael Nelson and the North American Association of State and Provincial Lotteries, do you believe that state governments should hold lotteries? Should they use advertising to encourage participation in such lotteries? Defend your answer.

Chapter 2

1. In discussing whether compulsive gambling is an addiction, both Ronald M. Pavalko and Michael Walker compare it to drug addiction. How do their comparisons differ? In your opinion, whose analogy is more convincing?

2. Henry R. Lesieur uses many statistics to describe the costs associated with compulsive gambling, while Nick Gillespie relies more on anecdotes to support his claim that compulsive gambling is not as widespread as antigambling activists claim. Whose argument do you find more convincing, and why?

3. The American Gaming Association (AGA) denies that the gambling industry preys on compulsive gamblers, as Bernard P. Horn claims. How does the fact that AGA represents the casino industry affect your evaluation of the association's arguments?

Chapter 3

1. What social costs does the *Economist* claim are caused by legalized gambling? Do you find Frank J. Fahrenkopf Jr.'s denial of these costs persuasive? Why or why not?

2. The Economics Resource Group (ERG) describes the spread of Indian casinos as an enormously beneficial development for Native Americans, while David Pace points out that Indian gaming has disappointed many tribes. Based on the two viewpoints, do you agree with the ERG's assessment that "the positive social and economic aspects of [Indian] gaming . . . far outweigh the negative"? Why or why not?

Chapter 4

1. Timothy A. Kelly believes it is time for a federal moratorium on gambling expansion, while Guy Calvert feels that the government should not curtail or prohibit an activity that the majority of Americans enjoy. Whose argument do you find more persuasive, and why? What is your own opinion of the government's role in restricting or prohibiting gambling?

2. Based on the viewpoints by Jon Kyl and Tom W. Bell, do you think the government should make gambling on the Internet illegal? Defend your answer using quotes from the viewpoints.

3. Do you find James C. Dobson's argument that a nationwide ban on college sports betting would reduce point-shaving scandals and underage gambling persuasive, or do you agree with Danny Sheridan that such a ban would only exacerbate these problems? Explain your answer.

Organizations to Contact

The editors have compiled the following list of organizations concerned with the issues debated in this book. The descriptions are derived from materials provided by the organizations. All have publications or information available for interested readers. The list was compiled on the date of publication of the present volume; the information provided here may change. Be aware that many organizations take several weeks or longer to respond to inquiries, so allow as much time as possible.

American Gaming Association
555 13th St. NW, Suite 1010 East, Washington, DC 20004
(202) 637-6500
website: www.americangaming.org

The American Gaming Association (AGA) represents the commercial casino entertainment industry. It informs the general public, elected officials, and other decision makers about the gaming industry. It also lobbies for and against federal legislation affecting tourism, gambling regulations, and other matters. AGA publishes two newsletters, *The Responsible Gaming Resource Guide*, and several studies, including *Casinos and Crime: An Analysis of the Evidence* and *The Economic Impacts of Casino Gaming in the United States*.

Cato Institute
1000 Massachusetts Ave. NW, Washington, DC 20001
(202) 842-0200 • fax: (202) 842-3490

The Cato Institute is a libertarian public-policy research foundation. It evaluates government policies and offers reform proposals and commentary on its website. Its publications include the Cato Policy Analysis series of reports, which have included *Gambling America: Balancing the Risks of Gambling and Its Regulation* and *Internet Gambling: Popular, Inexorable, and (Eventually) Legal*. It also publishes the magazines *Regulation* and the *Cato Policy Report*.

Common Cause
1250 Connecticut Ave. NW, Suite 600, Washington, DC 20036
(202) 833-1200
website: www.commoncause.org

Common Cause is a nonprofit, nonpartisan citizens' lobbying organization promoting open, honest, and accountable government. The organization works to curb the influence of money and special interests on public officials. Common Cause regularly publishes investigative studies, such as *Gamblers Unanimous*, on the effects of money in politics and reports on a variety of ethics and integrity-in-government issues.

Family Research Council
801 G St. NW, Washington, DC 20001
(202) 393-2100
website: www.frc.org

The Family Research Council (FRC) works to promote traditional family and Judeo-Christian principles on a national scale, particularly in Washington, D.C. It promotes and defends traditional family values in print, broadcast, and other media outlets and advocates legislative and public-policy initiatives to strengthen the traditional family. FRC opposes the spread of legalized gambling. The organization publishes a newsletter, *Family Policy* magazine, and the Insight series of policy analysis papers.

Focus on the Family
Colorado Springs, CO 80995
(719) 531-5181
website: www.family.org

Focus on the Family is a Christian ministry working to help preserve traditional values and the institution of the family. It publishes *Focus on the Family* magazine, which has included articles such as "Room, Board & Bookies: The Perils of Student Gambling," as well as many books and videos that address public-policy and cultural issues. The CitizenLink section of Focus on the Family's website contains many fact sheets on the harms associated with gambling, including "Gambling and Crime," "Gambling and the Bible," and "Gambling and Suicide."

Gamblers Anonymous
PO Box 17173, Los Angeles, CA 90017
(213) 386-8789
website: www.gamblersanonymous.org

Gamblers Anonymous (GA) is a fellowship of men and women who share with each other their experience, strength, and hope that they may solve their common problem and help others with gambling problems. Gamblers Anonymous does not wish to engage in any controversy and neither endorses nor opposes any cause. Its members' primary goal is to stop gambling and help other compulsive gamblers do the same. On its website, GA provides a list of twenty questions gamblers can use to assess whether they have a problem, and includes an overview of the twelve steps GA members use to overcome their problem.

Harvard Medical School Division on Addiction
350 Longwood Ave., Suite 200, Boston, MA 02115
(617) 432-0058
websites: www.hms.harvard.edu/doa • www.thewager.com

The mission of the Division on Addiction at Harvard Medical School is to strengthen worldwide understanding of addiction through innovative research, education, and the global exchange of information. It publishes the *Journal of Gambling Studies* and reports such as *Estimating the Prevalence of Disordered Gambling in the United States and Canada: A Meta-Analysis* and *Gambling, Drinking, Smoking, and Other Health Risk Activities Among Casino Employees*. It also maintains *The WAGER* (*Weekly Addiction Gambling Educational Report*), a free online publication devoted to increasing the accessibility of gambling-related research and news.

Institute for the Study of Gambling and Commercial Gaming
College of Business Administration, University of Nevada, Reno, NV 89557
(702) 784-1110
website: www.unr.edu/gaming/index.asp

The institute offers courses and degrees in management and other areas of gambling. It holds national and international conferences on gambling and publishes proceedings from them. The institute produces quarterly reports on current issues and trends in legalized gambling and copublishes, with the National Council on Problem Gambling, the quarterly *Journal of Gambling Studies*.

National Center for Responsible Gaming
PO Box 25366, Kansas City, MO 64119-0666
(816) 453-9964
website: www.ncrg.org

The National Center for Responsible Gaming (NCRG) is a national organization exclusively devoted to funding scientific research on pathological and youth gambling. NCRG-sponsored researchers improve strategies for the prevention and treatment of problem gambling. The council publishes annual reports, press releases, and information on the technical publications that NCRG investigators have authored.

National Coalition Against Legalized Gambling
100 Maryland Ave., Room 311, Washington, DC 20002
(800) 664-2680
website: www.ncalg.org

The National Coalition Against Legalized Gambling (NCALG) is concerned with the rapid expansion of gambling across the country, especially with gambling's addictive effect on youth, families, and governments. It opposes the gambling industry in every forum at every level with every educational tool available. NCALG provides information, research, and technical support to state groups battling the expansion of gambling. Its website acts as an antigambling clearinghouse and information center, providing news updates, testimony from NCALG officials, and fact sheets such as "The Case Against Legalized Gambling" and "The Negative Economic Impact of Casinos."

National Congress of American Indians (NCAI)
900 Pennsylvania Ave. SE, Washington, DC 20003
(202) 546-9404
website: www.ncai.org

NCAI is an organization of tribes representing six hundred thousand Indians that seeks to protect, conserve, and develop Indian natural and human resources. It believes that gaming is a right of Native American tribes and an aspect of tribal sovereignty. It also believes that the 1988 Indian Gaming Regulatory Act (IGRA) was a concession to the federal government and states and that further concessions are unwarranted. NCAI publishes a quarterly newsletter, the *Sentinel*.

National Council on Problem Gambling
208 G St. NE, Washington, DC 20002
(202) 547-9204
website: www.ncpgambling.org

The mission of the National Council on Problem Gambling is to increase public awareness of pathological gambling, increase treatment for problem gamblers and their families, and encourage research and programs for prevention and education. The council publishes informational pamphlets such as "Problem and Pathological Gambling in America" and "When Someone You Love Gambles."

National Gambling Impact Study Commission
800 North Capitol St. NW, Suite 450, Washington, DC 20002
website: www.ngisc.gov

The National Gambling Impact Study Commission (NGISC) was created by Congress and President Bill Clinton to conduct a comprehensive legal and factual study of the social and economic impacts of gambling on federal, state, local, and Native American tribal governments. The commission issued its final report in June

1999. Among its recommendations were that the federal government ban Internet gambling and state governments institute a moratorium on further gambling expansion. The full report is available on the NGISC website.

National Indian Gaming Association
224 Second St. SE, Washington, DC 20003
(202) 546-7711
website: www.niga.org

The National Indian Gaming Association (NIGA) is a nonprofit organization of 168 Indian nations engaged in tribal gaming enterprises. NIGA's mission is to protect and preserve the general welfare of tribes striving for self-sufficiency through gaming enterprises. The association works with the federal government and Congress to develop sound policies and practices and to provide technical assistance and advocacy on gaming-related issues. It publishes a newsletter, several informational videos, and *The Indian Gaming Handbook*. Its website also offers numerous testimonies from tribal leaders on the benefits of Indian gaming, as well as reports such as *American Indian Gaming Policy and Its Socio-Economic Effects*.

North American Association of State and Provincial Lotteries
2775 Bishop Rd., Suite B, Willoughby Hills, OH 44092
(216) 241-2310
website: www.naspl.org

The North American Association of State and Provincial Lotteries (NASPL) represents forty-six lottery organizations throughout North America. It assembles and disseminates information and benefits of state and provincial lottery organizations. NASPL's website contains a list of frequently asked questions on problem gambling, an overview of lottery history, and a list of the various government and charitable organizations that lottery proceeds benefit.

Responsible Gaming Council
505 Consumers Rd., Suite 801, Toronto, ON M2J 4V8 Canada
(416) 499-9800
website: www.responsiblegambling.org

An organization of business and health professionals and others, the Responsible Gaming Council provides executive summaries of surveys of Ontario residents' attitudes and behavior regarding gambling. It publishes pamphlets on compulsive gambling and teen gambling and has produced a high school curriculum and educational video about problem gambling.

United Methodist Church General Board of Church and Society

100 Maryland Ave. NE, Washington, DC 20002
(202) 488-5600 / (800) 967-0880
website: www.umc-gbcs.org

This department of the United Methodist Church believes that "gambling is a menace to society; deadly to the best interests of moral, social, economic, and spiritual life; and destructive of good government." It urges Christians and others to abstain from gambling and opposes state promotion and legalization of gambling. The board provides an antigambling information packet that includes position papers, pamphlets, and article reprints.

Bibliography of Books

Thomas Barker and Marjie Britz

Jokers Wild: Legalized Gambling in the Twenty-First Century. Westport, CT: Praeger, 2000.

Frederick Barthelme

Double Down: Reflections on Gambling and Loss. Boston: Houghton Mifflin, 1999.

Jeff Benedict

Without Reservation: The Making of America's Most Powerful Indian Tribe and the World's Largest Casino. New York: HarperCollins, 2000.

Linda Berman and Mary-Ellen Siegel

Behind the 8-Ball: A Guide for Families of Gamblers. New York: Simon & Schuster, 1992.

Tyler Bridges

Bad Bet on the Bayou: The Rise of Gambling in Louisiana and the Fall of Governor Edwin Edwards. New York: Farrar, Straus and Giroux, 2001.

Jeff Burbank

License to Steal: Nevada's Gaming Control System in the Megaresort Age. Las Vegas: University of Nevada Press, 2000.

Brian Castellani

Pathological Gambling: The Making of a Medical Problem. Albany: State University of New York Press, 2000.

Linda L. Chamberlain

Best Possible Odds: Contemporary Treatment Strategies for Gambling Disorders. New York: John Wiley & Sons, 2000.

D. Kirk Davidson

Selling Sin: The Marketing of Socially Unacceptable Products. Westport, CT: Quorum Books, 1996.

Sally Denton and Roger Morris

The Money and the Power: The Making of Las Vegas and Its Hold on America. New York: Knopf, 2001.

Pete Earley

Super Casino: Inside the "New" Las Vegas. New York: Bantam Books, 2000.

Kim Isaac Eisler

Revenge of the Pequots: How a Small Native American Tribe Created the World's Most Profitable Casino. New York: Simon & Schuster, 2001.

Rod L. Evans and Mark Hence, eds.

Legalized Gambling: For and Against. Chicago: Open Court, 1998.

Ronald A. Farrell

The Black Book and the Mob: The Untold Story of the Control of Nevada's Casinos. Madison: University of Wisconsin Press, 1995.

John M. Findlay	*People of Chance: Gambling in American Society from Jamestown to Las Vegas*. New York: Oxford University Press, 1986.
Robert Goodman	*The Luck Business: The Devastating Consequences and Broken Promises of America's Gambling Explosion*. New York: Free Press, 1995.
Mary Heineman	*Losing Your Shirt: Recovery for Compulsive Gamblers and Their Families*. Center City, MN: Hazelden, 2001.
Cathy H.C. Hsu, ed.	*Legalized Casino Gaming in the United States: The Economic and Social Impact*. Binghamton, NY: Haworth Hospitality Press, 1999.
David Neil Isaacs	*You Bet Your Life: The Burdens of Gambling*. Lexington: University of Kentucky Press, 2001.
Bettina L. Knapp	*Gambling, Game, and Psyche*. Albany: State University of New York Press, 2000.
Ambrose I. Lane	*Return of the Buffalo*. Westport, CT: Bergin & Garvey, 1995.
W. Dale Mason	*Indian Gaming: Tribal Sovereignty and American Politics*. Norman: University of Oklahoma Press, 2000.
Richard McGowan	*State Lotteries and Legalized Gambling: Painless Revenue or Painful Mirage*. Westport, CT: Quorum, 1994.
Jan McMillen, ed.	*Gambling Cultures: Studies in History and Interpretation*. New York: Routledge, 1996.
Roger Munting	*An Economic and Social History of Gambling in Britain and the USA*. Manchester and New York: Manchester University Press, 1996.
David Nibert	*Hitting the Lottery Jackpot: State Government and the Taxing of Dreams*. New York: Monthly Review Press, 2000.
Timothy L. O'Brien	*Bad Bet: The Inside Story of the Glamour, Glitz, and Danger of America's Gambling Industry*. New York: Times Business, 1998.
Ronald M. Pavalko	*Problem Gambling and Its Treatment: An Introduction*. Springfield, IL: Charles C. Thomas, 2001.
Richard Sasuly	*Bookies and Bettors: Two Hundred Years of Gambling*. New York: Holt, Rinehart, and Winston, 1982.

David Spanier	*Inside the Gambler's Mind*. Reno: University of Nevada Press, 1994.
David Spanier	*Welcome to the Pleasure Dome: Inside Las Vegas*. Reno: University of Nevada Press, 1992.
Jennifer Vogel, ed.	*Crapped Out: How Gambling Ruins the Economy and Destroys Lives*. Monroe, ME: Common Courage Press, 1997.
Michael Walker	*The Psychology of Gambling*. Oxford, NY: Pergamon Press, 1992.

Index